WHAT IS TRUTH FOR?

'Everyone claims to care about truth – yet surprisingly few are really dedicated to pursuing it, which requires not just freedom but virtues like integrity, self-discipline, and humility. N.J. Enfield explains how each of us can become a better truth-seeker – and, in doing so, become a better person, too.'
Jonathan Rauch, Brookings Institution

'Truth needs its champions these days, and N.J. Enfield rises to the challenge. This punchy volume reveals what truth is, how best to go about finding it, and why it's okay if we never perfectly achieve it. A bracing corrective at a time when truth is being called into question more than ever.'
Sean Carroll, Johns Hopkins University

'Drawing upon multiple disciplines and real-world examples, Enfield demonstrates that robust free speech is the essential engine for pursuing truth.'
Nadine Strossen, New York Law School

'Top-drawer linguistics meets Truth, and finds that it's small-t, yet essential. When used well, the word "truth" has rhetorical power.'
Deirdre McCloskey, economist

The status quo is broken. The world is grappling with a web of challenges that could threaten our very existence. If we believe in a better world, now is the time to question the purpose behind our actions and those taken in our name.

Enter the What Is It For? series – a bold exploration of the core elements shaping our world, from religion and free speech to animal rights and war. This series cuts through the noise to reveal the true impact of these topics, what they really do and why they matter.

Ditching the usual heated debates and polarizations, this series offers fresh, forward-thinking insights. Leading experts present groundbreaking ideas and point to ways forward for real change, urging us to envision a brighter future.

Each book dives into the history and function of its subject, uncovering its role in society and, crucially, how it can be better.

Series editor: George Miller

Visit **bristoluniversitypress.co.uk/what-is-it-for** to find out more about the series.

Available now

WHAT ARE ANIMAL RIGHTS FOR?
Steve Cooke

WHAT IS COUNTERTERRORISM FOR?
Leonie Jackson

WHAT IS CYBERSECURITY FOR?
Tim Stevens

WHAT IS DRUG POLICY FOR?
Julia Buxton

WHAT IS HISTORY FOR?
Robert Gildea

WHAT IS HUMANISM FOR?
Richard Norman

WHAT IS JOURNALISM FOR?
Jon Allsop

WHAT IS THE MONARCHY FOR?
Laura Clancy

WHAT ARE MUSEUMS FOR?
Jon Sleigh

WHAT ARE THE OLYMPICS FOR?
Jules Boykoff

WHAT IS PHILANTHROPY FOR?
Rhodri Davies

WHAT ARE PRISONS FOR?
Hindpal Singh Bhui

WHAT IS TRUTH FOR?
N.J. Enfield

WHAT IS VEGANISM FOR?
Catherine Oliver

WHAT IS WAR FOR?
Jack McDonald

WHAT IS THE WELFARE STATE FOR?
Paul Spicker

WHAT ARE ZOOS FOR?
Heather Browning and Walter Veit

Forthcoming

WHAT IS ANARCHISM FOR?
Nathan Jun

WHAT IS ANTHROPOLOGY FOR?
Kriti Kapila

WHAT ARE CONSPIRACY THEORIES FOR?
James Fitzgerald

WHAT IS FIFA FOR?
Alan Tomlinson

WHAT IS FREE SPEECH FOR?
Gavan Titley

WHAT IS IMMIGRATION POLICY FOR?
Madeleine Sumption

WHAT IS INTERNATIONAL DEVELOPMENT FOR?
Andrea Cornwall

WHAT ARE MARKETS FOR?
Phillip Roscoe

WHAT IS MUSIC FOR?
Fleur Brouwer

WHAT ARE NUCLEAR WEAPONS FOR?
Patricia Shamai

WHAT ARE THE POLICE FOR?
Ben Bradford

WHAT IS RELIGION FOR?
Malise Ruthven

WHAT IS RESILIENCE FOR?
Hamideh Mahdiani

WHAT IS SPACE EXPLORATION FOR?
Tony Milligan and Koji Tachibana

WHAT ARE STATUES FOR?
Milly Williamson

N.J. ENFIELD is Professor of Linguistics at the University of Sydney. His award-winning research on how language influences the ways we think and act has been published widely in linguistics, anthropology and cognitive science, as well as in the media. He is a member of the Fighting Truth Decay research node at the Charles Perkins Centre.

WHAT IS TRUTH FOR?

N.J. ENFIELD

First published in Great Britain in 2025 by

Bristol University Press
University of Bristol
1–9 Old Park Hill
Bristol
BS2 8BB
UK
t: +44 (0)117 374 6645
e: bup-info@bristol.ac.uk

Details of international sales and distribution partners are available at
bristoluniversitypress.co.uk

© N.J. Enfield 2025

British Library Cataloguing in Publication Data
A catalogue record for this book is available from the British Library

ISBN 978-1-5292-4938-5 paperback
ISBN 978-1-5292-4939-2 ePub
ISBN 978-1-5292-4940-8 ePdf

The right of N.J. Enfield to be identified as author of this work has been asserted
by him in accordance with the Copyright, Designs and Patents Act 1988.

All rights reserved: no part of this publication may be reproduced, stored in
a retrieval system, or transmitted in any form or by any means, electronic,
mechanical, photocopying, recording, or otherwise without the prior permission of
Bristol University Press.

Every reasonable effort has been made to obtain permission to reproduce
copyrighted material. If, however, anyone knows of an oversight, please contact
the publisher.

The statements and opinions contained within this publication are solely those of the
author and not of the University of Bristol or Bristol University Press. The University
of Bristol and Bristol University Press disclaim responsibility for any injury to
persons or property resulting from any material published in this publication.

Bristol University Press works to counter discrimination on grounds of gender,
race, disability, age and sexuality.

Cover design: Tom Appshaw

I dedicate this book to the memory of my father, John David Enfield. This is my first book written since I passed the age that he was at the end of his life. Now I see that every new day is a gift.

Human knowledge and human power come to the same thing, because ignorance of cause frustrates effect.
>	Francis Bacon, 1620

Man is perfectible, or in other words susceptible of perpetual improvement.
>	William Godwin, 1793

I may be wrong and you may be right, and by an effort, we may get nearer to the truth.
>	Karl Popper, 1945

CONTENTS

List of Figures		xvi
Acknowledgements		xviii
Preface		xx
1	**Is There Snow on Mount Everest?**	1
2	**True Statements are Good Reasons**	16
3	**The Two Realities**	27
4	**Collateral Effects**	43
5	**Always Striving, Never Arriving**	61
6	**The Ostrich Instruction**	82
7	**Mindful Optimism**	97
Notes		110
Further Reading		123
Index		124

LIST OF FIGURES

0.1 Detail of a French cannon outside the Museum of Military History, Vienna, Austria (reproduced under the terms of the GNU Free Documentation License) — xx

1.1 Thomas Becket being murdered by four knights in Canterbury Cathedral on 29 December 1170. From *Cassell's Illustrated History of England*, Volume 1 (Cassell, Petter & Galpin, 1865) (public domain) — 5

2.1 Illustrations from John Ashton's *The Devil in Britain and America* (1896), purporting to show women engaged in witchcraft: having commerce with a devil and brewing a witches' broth (Ward and Downey, 1896) (public domain) — 25

3.1 The Eucharist – a priest elevates the host during mass. Photograph by Josh Applegate, 2019 (reproduced under Unsplash licence) — 30

3.2 Matriarch of Ahoe ethnicity, Mrs Khamsone, at her home in Sop Hia Village, Central Laos. Photograph by N.J. Enfield, 17 August 2010 — 39

4.1 'The Followers of Christ's cemetery is full of graves marking the deaths of children who lived a day, a week, a month.' Photograph — 52

	by Jason Wilson for the *Guardian* (reproduced with permission)	
4.2	Isaac Mwaura with Bianca Chacha and Gabriel Kinyanjui. Photograph by Lydia Matata (courtesy of *Global Press Journal*)	54
5.1	Popeye, spinach advocate extraordinaire. E.C. Segar (public domain)	67
5.2	At full moon, the gravitational pulls of the sun and moon are aligned, their 'forces are conjoined' (Newton) causing spring tides	75
5.3	At half-moon, the gravitational pulls of the sun and moon compete, 'the difference of their forces' (Newton) causing neap tides	76
6.1	London tube map, 1908 (public domain)	93
7.1	Jazz musician Sidney Bechet, New York, *c.* November 1946. William P. Gottlieb/Ira and Leonore S. Gershwin Fund Collection, Music Division, Library of Congress (public domain)	103

ACKNOWLEDGEMENTS

I am extremely grateful for generous comments from many people who were kind enough to provide input, commentary and discussion on the ideas discussed in this book. These include Gareth Baker, Julie Cairns, Margaret Enfield, Martin Fahy, Peter Fray, Martin Haspelmath, Julia Kindt, Wassim Kisirwani, George Miller, Tibor Molnar, Steven Pinker, Michael Rich, J.P. de Ruiter, Jack Sexton, Caroline West, Colin Wight, Samantha Williams and Peter Wilson. I am especially grateful to George Miller at Bristol University Press for suggesting that I write this book, and for his advice along the way.

I have drawn on some earlier publications: Some paragraphs of Chapter 6 are revised sections from an article published in the Australian Farm Institute's Farm Policy Journal: http://farminstitute.org.au/publications/journal/farm-policy-journal-winter-2020. I am grateful for permission to publish these. I have also included revised versions of some lines from two reviews published in the *Times Literary Supplement*: N.J. Enfield, 'Big Tech Is Reading Your Mind: Software Engineers Have Become Social Engineers in Our Democracies', *The Times Literary Supplement*, 13 January 2023; and N.J. Enfield, 'Believe What You

ACKNOWLEDGEMENTS

Like: How We Fit the Facts Around Our Prejudices', *The Times Literary Supplement*, 17 July 2021.

PREFACE

Truth is for striving at, for the sake of good collective action.

Truth matters because the world is real. It matters because we will never be exempt from the final argument of nature: *Ultima ratio naturae*. I borrow this phrasing from the words that Louis XIV, 17th-century king of France, had cast on the cannons of his armies: *Ultima ratio regum*, 'The Final Argument of Kings' (see Figure 0.1).

Figure 0.1: Detail of a French cannon outside the Museum of Military History, Vienna, Austria

If the king fails to prevail by persuasion or threat, he will resort to brute force, drawing on natural causes. Nature provides the force that will, one day, unflinchingly prevail over us all, kings included. But until then, nature's final arguments can be studied, reasoned with, and even held at bay. Knowledge is our key to longevity.

Take the simple example of toxic plants, a challenge that humans have faced since the dawn of our species. Plants are an abundant source of food. How do we know which plants are good to eat, and which are dangerous? One method is trial and error. But that can be costly, given that eating the wrong plant might send you to hospital or even the morgue. We avoid error with knowledge, and we acquire knowledge mostly from other people. I know which plants are good to eat because I've been told by those who know, and I have trusted those who know because we are part of a cohesive, cooperative social group. This coordination around knowledge is made possible by language, our species' great invention. But with language, there's a problem. People can say things that aren't true.

Suppose you are on a field trip to a remote village in the mountain tops near the Laos–Vietnam border.[1] Your host, a local villager, prepares a meal using a wild tuber, a bulbous section of plant root dug from the ground. You are aware that many species of tuber, such as *Dioscorea hispida*, are highly toxic. But you are told, through a translator, 'This one is safe to eat'.

The statement raises the two-part *alignment problem* that has been with us since the innovation of language itself.[2] First, is the statement aligned with the speaker's belief? You hope they're not trying to deceive you, and that they are sincere when they tell that you the food is safe. Second, is the statement aligned with the facts? The villager might be genuinely mistaken. If that's the case, you eat the meal and become dangerously ill, the last thing you want in the wilds of Laos.

The idea of truth gives us an incentive to heed this twin alignment principle. How can we achieve this? The answer is by using the gift of optimistic reasoning. By 'optimism', I do not mean the everyday wishful thought that everything will be all right. That, paradoxically, is a dangerous stance that causes us to switch off our critical faculties, more likely making things worse. By optimism here I mean something different, and much better. This sense of optimism provides the foundational incentive to seek understanding and know the truth. It has its roots in 18th-century anarchist philosopher William Godwin's doctrine of the *perpetual perfectibility* of humankind. An optimist believes that improvement is always possible. An optimist wants to learn, wants to be corrected, wants to revise and refine their beliefs. This yearning for improvement creates a natural tendency towards the twin alignment that keeps nature's cannons away.

Optimism is the view that anything you want to do will either be 'impossible because it is forbidden by the laws of nature' or 'achievable, given the right knowledge', as physicist David Deutsch has put it.[3] If we want to solve problems, we can't change the laws of nature. So, our task is to find the needed knowledge.

Consequently, Deutsch says, 'all evils are caused by insufficient knowledge'.[4] And conversely, knowledge enables the opposites of evil: freedom, creativity and progress. We who are alive today enjoy the benefits of our ancestors' extraordinary successes in learning how nature works (see Chapter 5). Natural human curiosity and wit have allowed us to amass cultural knowledge for tens of millennia, and in recent centuries this process has been supercharged by the scientific mindset captured in the slogan *Sapere aude*, 'Dare to know' (attributed to the Roman poet Horace, 65 BC–8 BC, and used by philosopher Immanuel Kant in his famous 1784 essay, 'What is Enlightenment?').

A counterpoint to radical optimism is mysterianism, the idea that just as cats can't do calculus, there are things we humans simply cannot know.[5] In this book, we favour the optimists, for the following reason. Mysterianism risks being an off-switch: there are things we can't know, so why try? Optimism is the antidote, a great on-switch for creative thinking, constructive critique and collective error-correction.

While the truth itself is elusive, the ideal of truth as a target is supremely useful. If we do not strive for truth, our decisions will be unmoored, risky at best, often foolish, and sometimes fatal. But such folly can be avoided. Truth is the best device we have for effectively coordinating our decisions and actions. Truth is an ancient problem and we will always need to solve it. In the chapters that follow, we explore the ingredients of a mindful, pragmatic and optimistic approach to truth.

Nature is an indifferent tyrant. One day, its laws will end our time on earth. This means that knowing the facts and heeding them are more important than anything. How do we do this? There is no technical solution. It can't be fixed by fancy apps, fact-checkers or legislation. The only effective device for navigating, analysing and gatekeeping in the quest for truth – more accurately, the quest to eliminate error – is a community of mindful, disciplined, humble and critical thinkers who want to know the truth more than they want to be right. We must all be those people.

This book argues for a culture of truth-seeking, error-correction and optimism. It argues for real creativity combined with real tolerance of criticism, and for humility in the face of challenging possibilities. Nature's cannons are loaded and always aimed, and knowledge is our only defence against them. When reality intervenes, beliefs must change. And the more grounded in reality our shared beliefs, the more we flourish. That's what truth is for.

1
IS THERE SNOW ON MOUNT EVEREST?

> Truth is a property of statements, not a property of the
> world. This makes language central in the quest for truth.

Who would deny that there is snow on Mount Everest? As the philosopher John Searle has said, it's a 'brute fact'.[1] I agree that there is snow on Everest, but what are we saying when we say it's true? We are making a claim, in the form of a statement, in a language. In this case, English.

To find out if the claim of snow on Everest is true, we could travel to the great mountain and see for ourselves. But it is not enough just to check the way the world is. When we test the truth of a statement, we are looking to see if the world matches with the words that claim to describe it. For that, in the snow on Everest example, we need to make reference to the English language. We need to know the meanings of English words like *snow* and *on*. This may seem trivial. But defining words is harder than it looks. More importantly, there are thousands of languages on Earth, most of which don't have words that mean exactly what *snow* (or indeed most other words) means in English. (And not only that, even the little word *on* cannot be translated directly into many languages of the world.)

So, there may be cold, white stuff on Everest, but is it 'snow'? That question is as much about English as it is about Everest.

Just as facts are tested against language, language is tested against facts. The logician Alfred Tarski wrote: 'The sentence "Snow is white" is true if, and only if, snow is white'.[2] According to this view, the meanings of words can be discovered by going out into the world and checking what philosophers call their truth conditions. So, to test if the statement 'Snow is white' is true, just find some snow and see if it's white. Again, language intervenes. You need to know what counts as 'snow', and what counts as 'white'. Trivial? Only if you are wearing your English-language goggles and you are blissfully unaware that you are wearing them. There is no language-independent way to communicate a claim, or to agree that it is true.

This raises problems for anyone who wants to find the truth.

One issue is that a single word can mean different things. In dialects of English, one word has many meanings. The word *biscuit* may refer to a small, soft cake, a crisp cracker, or a chocolate cream cookie, depending on where you are in the English-speaking world. Seeing the facts through language requires knowing which lens you are looking through.

Other examples are more obviously consequential.

Do you know what *aircraft* means? We might think first of a medium-sized passenger plane. But the term covers all fixed-wing flying machines, from the tiny 500-pound Starr Bumble Bee II to the 300-ton Antonov An-225. Now what about helicopters? Is it true to say that a helicopter is an aircraft? It turns out that this question can matter very much.

In April 1994, in northern Iraq, two US Army UH-60 Black Hawk helicopters were shot down and destroyed, killing 26 people, including military personnel and civilians.[3] They were destroyed by friendly fire. Two US Air Force F-15 fighter jets made the decision to shoot them down, guided by a US Air Force AWACS (Airborne Warning and Control System) airplane. The F-15 pilots mistakenly believed that the US Army helicopters were Iraqi Mi-24s, and the AWACS personnel did not exercise adequate control leading to the decision to fire. Among the many contributing causes of this complex incident, language played a role. Air Force personnel misidentified the helicopters as hostile, partly because they understood that no US aircraft should be in that area. But army and air force definitions of the word aircraft differ. For army aviators, helicopters are not aircraft, but for air force aviators, they are. This contributed to why the F-15 pilots misidentified the helicopters as hostile, and why the army aviators did not expect to be shot down.[4]

The actions of both sides were consistent with the understanding that no US 'aircraft' should have been flying in that area. But because of the ambiguity of that word in relation to helicopters, 26 people lost their lives.

This shows how important it can be to calibrate the meanings of words when evaluating whether what someone says is true. The aircraft/helicopter example illustrates the problem of ambiguity in words. Another kind of problem is the distinction between the literal meaning of what someone says and the intention that may be implied by it.

At Christmas in the year 1170, Henry II of England was at his castle at Bures in Normandy. He was venting his frustrations about the Archbishop of Canterbury, Thomas Becket, whose rogue behaviour was undermining support for Henry. Becket had excommunicated several bishops who were supportive of the king. Henry's outburst of frustration at the contempt shown by Becket went something like this: 'Will no one rid me of this meddlesome priest?'[5] Soon afterwards, four knights who had heard the king's words travelled to Canterbury where they confronted Becket and killed him (see Figure 1.1).

Were the four knights following an order? Henry's words certainly had that effect. But crucially, Henry could deny any claim that he had ordered the murder. That is, in a court of law, the king may be asked, 'Did you order the killing of Thomas Becket?' and he may answer, 'No, I merely voiced my frustration at his meddling.'

Figure 1.1: Thomas Becket being murdered by four knights in Canterbury Cathedral on 29 December 1170

In the Hollywood film *Wolf of Wall Street*, stockbroker Jordan Belfort, played by Leonardo DiCaprio, is talking to FBI investigator Patrick Denham, who is visiting Belfort's luxury yacht and has just informed Belfort that he is under criminal investigation for fraud.[6] Belfort asks Denham: 'What are you pulling, 50, 60k?' Denham asks what an intern at Belfort's firm makes. Belfort replies: 'North of half a million dollars. And … I'd do that for anybody, you know. Anybody that … needs the proper guidance.' Denham retorts: 'You just tried to bribe a federal officer.' Jordan replies: 'No, technically I didn't bribe anybody!' Jordan's last statement is a statement about language. He means that the words he used did not contain any literal offer of a bribe.

DiCaprio's character may be correct that a statement is not technically the same as a bribe, but he is skating on thin ice. Still, even if we can all agree that Belfort was offering a bribe, his actions were designed to evade that claim on a technicality of language, were the matter to reach a court of law. Deniability is an escape hatch in language. Things can be true under the radar, but if someone tries to point to them we can say they were never there.[7] In this way, we can say it is not true that Henry II ordered Becket's killing, even though we may suspect – like the four knights who carried out the deed – that that's precisely what Henry wanted.

Deniability can be invoked even in cases where intentions are communicated without words at all. In June 2007, US Republican senator Larry Craig, a long-time National Rifle Association Director, was detained in a men's bathroom in Minneapolis-St. Paul International Airport.[8] The police report states: 'At 1216 hours, Craig tapped his right foot. I recognized this as a signal used by persons wishing to engage in lewd conduct. Craig tapped his toes several times and moved his foot closer to my foot. I moved my foot up and down slowly.' Craig's tapping of the foot, and moving it across to the neighbouring stall, was taken as a signal meaning 'I want to engage in lewd conduct'. Was that true? Craig denied it, offering an alternative explanation for why his foot had ventured so far. He explained that he has 'a wide stance when going to the bathroom and that his foot may have touched mine'. Which account is the true one? It depends on our interpretation of the meaning of that foot movement.

And it is precisely the indirect, off-record, deniable nature of the foot movement that makes it suitable as an illegal or secretive signal.

Sometimes these indirect strategies are used out of politeness. Often, we say something that is, on the surface, a statement of fact, when actually it is intended to request assistance. Suppose we're in the kitchen and I say, 'I can't get this jar open'. It's a true statement, but am I just giving you a piece of information, or am I asking for your help? A global study of how people in different cultures recruit help in everyday life showed that this kind of indirect strategy is a human universal.[9] When people are having trouble getting something done, they often tell others about it. The result is that those others will often step in and help. The effect is the same, whether your problem is an overtight lid or an unruly archbishop.

The wiggle-room that language gives us can make the difference between carriage and miscarriage of justice. Legal decisions often depend on how terms are understood, as in the case of whether helicopters are aircraft. There are subtler ways in which the wordings of statements we accept can add up to a larger narrative.

In a rape case recorded in a municipal criminal court in the United States,[10] the defendant's attorney is questioning the plaintiff about the events of the evening leading up to the alleged rape. The attorney asks: 'Did he sit with you?' The plaintiff answers: 'He sat at our table.' Notice the difference between 'sat with us' versus 'sat at our table'. If the first is true, it suggests that the defendant was part of the social group, while the second refers only to the physical location where he was sitting. The plaintiff's wording is consistent with the claim that the defendant was not part of the group but was merely in the same place. Under oath, the plaintiff does not deny the truth of the claim that the accused was sitting at the same table as her. Indeed, as part of physical reality, that could be checked, say, by looking at CCTV records.

In this way, over and over, the plaintiff does not allow the attorney's words to stand as versions of the truth. Instead, she keeps offering alternative wordings that reject various implications that the defendant's attorney is carefully trying to insert into his account of the evening's events. The attorney describes the venue as a 'bar', the plaintiff corrects this to 'club'.[11] The attorney suggests that it's a place 'where girls and fellas meet', the plaintiff instead says 'people go there'. The attorney states 'you had lengthy conversations' with the accused, the plaintiff confirms only that 'we were all talking'. And the attorney asks, 'Did he take you out to the car?', to which the plaintiff responds 'No, he walked outside with us'.[12] See how, in fighting to establish the truth, she has to fight on so many fronts to block certain ways of characterizing the situation. Every inch she yields would allow a version of the truth that erodes her claim, or so the attorney hopes.

Why am I putting language in the foreground of a discussion about truth? Isn't truth about cold, hard facts? Why let words get in the way? Here is the reason. It is one thing for an individual to have a correct understanding of the reality around them. When an animal senses a threat and flees, a correct understanding of reality helps the creature survive. We are animals, so this applies to us. But our lives are both filled by, and shaped by, a *social* world, too. We are not just taking decisions and actions as individuals. We are coordinating those decisions and actions with others. And our go-to device for coordination is language. This means that we shift our attention from the world to the word. And the word conveys only the most stripped-back picture of the world.[13]

Reality allows almost infinite distinctions to be made. A simple example is the colour spectrum. The science of human visual perception shows that we can discriminate some two million just-noticeable differences in colour. Yet few languages have more than a handful of words for these shades and hues. This bluntness of language has the advantage of being economical. In most languages, one only has to learn a handful of colour terms, not two million. And there is of course a disadvantage to having only a handful of terms. Suppose I am in a paint store and you call me to ask if I could pick up some green paint that you need for a touch-up job on a chipped door frame. The problem is that you no longer have the label that specifies the exact shade of green you used and the paint store can supply thousands of shades that we could truthfully label as 'green' in English. Which exact shade do you want? Unless we share a highly specialized vocabulary – for example, if we know fancy words like *chartreuse*, *celadon* or *aquamarine*, or if we are familiar with a paint brand's specific labels, such as *olive leaf*, *herb planter* or *equatorial forest* – then language will fail us. If you simply say to get some 'green' paint, it is unlikely that I will get the shade you need, yet it will be true that the paint I buy is green.

The problem is compounded across languages. Some languages may allow you to be more specific than English, while most languages have even fewer colour distinctions. In relation to green, many languages have one word that covers both green and blue together, such as the Lao word *khiaw* or the Ancient Japanese word *ao*. In Laos or Ancient Japan, the paint store scenario would be even less likely to succeed.

To deal with this problem, language allows us to triangulate. If I am trying to describe the shade of green I need, my language gives me descriptors like *dark* or *light*. I can compare to objects whose specific colour is closer to what I want. A phrase like *light olive green* will greatly increase our chance of success. Triangulation helps close the gap between language and reality.

To understand the idea of triangulation, suppose you are trying to locate something in a landscape. If you have a single compass bearing to the object, it is not enough information to fix its location, as it could be anywhere along the line. But if you have compass bearings towards the object from multiple locations, you can more easily pinpoint its location. The analogy with words is this. A simple, one-word description of something may be true. But it may be so vague as to be of little use. But when you have multiple alternative descriptions of the same thing, together these different linguistic angles help you gain a more accurate understanding of what's being described.

Another way in which triangulation through language helps you get closer to the truth is by allowing you to remove extraneous, distracting information. Suppose you hear that a political leader has been assassinated. Who did it? You check the news. One site reports that it was the work of freedom fighters. Another says they were terrorists. Can these opposite-sounding statements both be objectively true? They can coexist because their meanings include inherently subjective components, which contain more opinion than fact. Freedom fighters are good, terrorists are bad, but beyond that they may be indistinguishable. An animal can be described as a dog, a companion or a mongrel, but which of these are 'true' descriptions depends less on any features of the animal than on the perspective of the person speaking.

When we acknowledge the central role that language plays in evaluating claims to truth, this raises a deeper question. If our claims to truth can only be framed in one or another of the thousands of languages spoken in the world today, is no absolute claim to truth possible? If there are alternative framings, are none of them objectively true? The answer is yes and no. Yes, it's true that when we try to coordinate our behaviour, we operate through the filter of whatever human language we happen to be speaking. And languages vary widely in the concepts and ideas they give us to work with. But no, as long as we are mindful of that variation, as long as we define our terms, and as long as we triangulate and look at the world through multiple vantage points, we can avoid being misdirected by language.

I am saying that truth and language are intertwined, but this does not mean that they are unmoored from reality. Whether I call it a truncheon, a night stick or a billy club, it will hurt like hell when it hits me in the head. Our words are only measures of reality. The underlying reality persists regardless.

To see that reality, we must be vigilant with our trust in words. There is a tendency to believe too easily in what words claim to mean. Consider the following statement: 'I was once a falcon.' In my case, this happens to be true, but out of context it seems mad. I was not a bird. I was a player in the Falcons rugby team. The example seems trivial because we would of course not be so naïve as to give language that sort of power. I'm not saying I was literally a falcon. But we are more easily led astray by words than we would like to think.

More than a century ago, early anthropologists in Europe were learning about the practices of cultures from far away.[14] One practice that fascinated them was totemism. This is where a society is separated into groups, each group being associated with an animal or other natural force, for example a snake, a falcon or a crow. Every individual belongs to one or another of these groups. This practice is similar to the use of 'houses' for organizing sport activities in schools. Belonging to a house creates permanent allegiances with one subgroup and rivalries against another.

In the early 1900s, French sociologist Émile Durkheim studied reports of totemic practices of Australian Aboriginal groups. He noted that groups across the continent used totemic labels. He took these labels quite literally. Durkheim suggested that being a member of one totemic group 'is presumed to entail an identity in nature'. A man of a given totem 'believes he is both a man in the usual sense of the word and an animal or plant of the totemic species'.[15] Durkheim suggested that humans and animals are united by totem identities, essences that are 'shared between people and animals of the same name', for example, 'crow'. On this view, a man is not just a member of the crow totem, he is, deep down, an actual crow.

This idea of totem identity – that when I say I'm a crow, I'm claiming that I really am a crow – seems like an old-fashioned caricature and is regarded as such by many modern anthropologists. But many still seem willing to interpret things literally. Was I really a falcon, just with the outward appearance of a boy? I may even have celebrated the metaphor with my teammates, with falcons as lightning-fast hunters capable of outmanoeuvring their prey. But it is just a metaphor. None of us had feathers, wings or beaks, nor could we fly.

Here is why I am raising this. Some may regard it as a mark of respect to cultural diversity not to question the truth claims of other groups of people. Once at an academic conference, I was speaking of an Indigenous group of Laos and their claims to be able to communicate with spirits that have supernatural powers. Perhaps to reassure the audience that I did not uncritically accept these claims, I remarked that of course the claims were not true. A sociology professor rebuked me: 'Who are we to question their epistemology?' While this sounds like a culturally supportive sentiment, it is a problem. This is the view that leads us to say that if someone says they are a crow, then we must grant that it's true ('for them'). And once we grant this kind of identity-based authority over truth claims, such claims cannot be disproven. Rather, they are regarded as true because the person who makes the claim has a special authority. That is, they become authoritarian. We can only hope that such claims are used for good. For example, claims about connections to spirits of geographical features have been invoked in successful land-rights claims by Indigenous people. This makes such claims useful, and positive in so far as they can create consequences that many may regard as good. But that does not make them true. Unfortunately, there is no guarantee that claims of access to spirits will be used for good, nor that they will be good for everyone involved. For every land-rights claim that invokes a supernatural claim by authority, there is a punitive witch accusation that does the same (as we shall see in Chapter 2).

We can agree to label a group of people as crows or falcons, and even sometimes talk as if they really were birds, for the purposes of organizing social life. But we had better not fall into believing that the claims are literally true. Language is flexible and multi-layered. Metaphors and other creative functions of language are everywhere. They have their uses. But they are obstacles for the student of truth.

Words can frame, misdirect, distract and mislead. Words matter, which is why we cannot let them go unexamined and uncontested. But do not believe that words have the magic to redefine brute reality. For words will not protect you from nature's cannons.

2
TRUE STATEMENTS ARE GOOD REASONS

> While all statements can stand as reasons for action, true statements are *good* reasons for action.

An elderly man named Kham lives in rural Laos, on the edge of a forest reserve. The first thing you notice is that he walks with a limp. He explains what happened. One day, before dawn, Kham set out with five other men, rifles in hand, to hunt the wild pigs that roam the forests and destroy their cassava crops. The men fanned out across the forest, moving forward hoping to corral any pigs and push them into view where they could be fired upon. When one of Kham's fellow hunters saw a pig move in the thick underbrush, he quickly aimed his rifle and pulled the trigger, only to find he had shot at Kham, hitting him in the leg. Kham recovered but the leg never fully healed. He has told the story a thousand times.

TRUE STATEMENTS ARE GOOD REASONS

The moral of Kham's story is that false belief can lead to ruin. Assertions and beliefs are seldom in the abstract. They have concrete consequences. They are always potential *reasons for action*. When our reasons are false, we risk harm, failure and waste. In Kham's example, the belief 'I see a pig in the underbrush' gave his neighbour a reason to fire his weapon. But the belief was false. It was a bad reason.

We need our reasons for action to be good,[1] and for that they need to be true, or as near to true as possible. This demands a certain mindset. Journalist and writer Julia Galef offers the military analogy of soldiers versus scouts.[2] We need to think like scouts: open-minded and unbiased seekers of actionable intelligence. A scout gathers information and returns to base to deliver the facts as best they can. The news they bring may be good or bad, convenient or inconvenient. But it had better be true or they will be putting their team in harm's way. By contrast, the soldier mindset is to take a position and defend it tooth and nail.

The soldier mindset is fuelled by the flaw in thinking known as confirmation bias. We naturally defend our position, even when we would be better off with a scout mindset. Only the well-informed scout will be ready to adjust to changing conditions, correct their own mistaken beliefs, and thereby increase their chances of success.

We often hear that the truth doesn't matter to people anymore. But this is mostly wrong. Our days are filled with decision after decision, and getting each one right will usually require us to know the truth.

WHAT IS TRUTH FOR?

The effects of not knowing the truth can range from minor inconvenience to major headache to utter ruin. Consider a few scenarios.

> You are planning to make a birthday cake for your daughter. You are at the supermarket, buying supplies for the task. You are sure that there are eggs at home, so you leave them off your shopping list. You get home to find that you were wrong. You have to go back to the store to buy the eggs.
>
> You are setting out on a long drive in a remote area. You glance at your fuel gauge. The needle indicates the tank is full. But in fact the indicator has stuck and your fuel tank is near empty. Fifty miles from anywhere, you run out of petrol and are stranded. You wait for hours and your day is ruined.
>
> Police officers visit your workplace and detain you. You are asked to appear in a line-up as part of a murder case. A murder witness identifies you as the killer. On their testimony, you are sentenced to life in prison. Thirty years later, DNA evidence exonerates you. You've lost half your life.
>
> Your right eye is diseased and cannot be fixed. The doctor orders that it be removed by a surgeon. You contemplate life with one eye. In the operating theatre, the surgeon removes the left eye, the healthy one, falsely believing it is the diseased one. Now you are fully blind.

TRUE STATEMENTS ARE GOOD REASONS

> Your friend, a chef, invites you to his home for dinner. He has cooked a sumptuous braised mushroom dish. You ask which mushrooms he has used. He replies that they are paddy straw mushrooms, bought fresh from a farmer's market. In fact, neither he nor the vendor knew that they were death caps. It is the last meal of your life.

Each of these stories has happened in real life. For the people in these scenarios, the truth mattered very much, and they all would wish they had known it.

So, truth can't be shrugged off. It's not the case that people these days don't care about the truth. But still we must admit that the cynic has a point. Sometimes, it is true, it really doesn't much matter if your belief is false. In the example of the mushroom meal, suppose the chef was mistaken about the species of mushroom but the mushrooms themselves were edible and harmless. Or in the case of the fuel gauge, suppose the fuel level was lower than you thought but happened not to run empty before you discovered the fault and could reach a petrol station. In those cases, the false belief happens not to matter but only because no adverse consequences occurred.

The fundamental problem in these scenarios is that our beliefs are *reasons for action*, and when those beliefs are false, we court disaster.

This is not just an issue in human affairs. In nature, beliefs are reasons for action too. When a male moth detects the odour of a female moth's mating pheromones, he has a reason to approach her. But nature has evolved forms of deception to exploit this.

The bolas spider releases an odour just like the female moth's mating pheromones.[3] It is so similar that male moths are deceived. They act on false reasons and pay with their lives.

Given stakes like these, we have ample incentive to be vigilant about truth, to be careful not to assume that our beliefs are accurate, and to double-check the facts at every turn. But there are counterforces. One is sheer efficiency. It's too costly to double-check every single assumption, and there is always time pressure. In the pig-hunting example, Kham's neighbour had to act fast or risk missing his chance.

Another counterforce to vigilance concerns people's motivations for saying the things they say, and our motivations for rejecting or believing them. Suppose Kim is talking to a friend about a mutual acquaintance named Abby. Kim says Abby has been drinking too much and is a danger to herself. Why is Kim saying this and should her friend believe her? The answers may have less to do with the facts of the matter than with the social function that Kim's statement serves. Maybe it is negative gossip, with Kim trying to get her friend on side against Abby.[4] Or maybe Kim is trying to show that she has a special concern for Abby, and expressing fear for her serves this function.[5] Both of these motivations, one negative, one positive, might encourage Kim to embellish the truth and portray Abby's behaviour as worse than it is. Either scenario illustrates how the truth can take second place to social motivations, a collateral effect we explore further in Chapter 4.

TRUE STATEMENTS ARE GOOD REASONS

Nineteenth-century philosopher William Clifford argued that believing something without evidence was morally wrong.[6] One reason is that it may lead to harmful consequences, as we have seen. Another is that it may harm a broader culture in which members of society value well-founded knowledge: 'The danger to society is not merely that it should believe wrong things, though that is great enough; but that it should become credulous, and lose the habit of testing things and inquiring into them.'[7] Along similar lines, political scientist Ilya Somin states that 'public ignorance is a type of pollution',[8] eroding our capacity to think critically and vote wisely.

The problem here is not only related to flawed habits of reasoning. It is also cultural and political. The less tolerant we are of people challenging others' beliefs (a cultural issue), the more susceptible we are to the brute authority of powerful people who may pronounce certain assertions to be true (a political issue). And those who suffer the consequences of unevidenced pronouncements are invariably those at the bottom of the ladder of power.

In the late 1990s, a young Indigenous Mayan woman of Guatemala named Nikte' Sis Iboy was trained in techniques of linguistic analysis. Her teacher, linguist Nora England of the University of Texas, wanted to empower Indigenous people to develop and revitalize their endangered languages.[9] Sis Iboy was a member of the Achi-speaking Mayan group of Guatemala. She was brought up to believe that her language was entirely separate from a neighbouring Indigenous language called K'ichee'. The two communities found it important to maintain ethnic and political independence from each other, and language had become a symbol of their distinctness.

With her training in the techniques of linguistic analysis, Sis Iboy gained the knowledge and agency to be able to evaluate evidence independently. She analysed the two languages – Achi and K'ichee' – and discovered that they were far closer to each other than she had believed. She found that they were dialects of a single language, and not separate languages at all.[10] As Nora England explained, Sis Iboy also had political motivations, as she 'came to believe that it is necessary to unify Mayan languages as much as possible if they are to be adequate modern means of communication that can hold their own against Spanish'. But when Sis Iboy tried to advance this idea, she was accused by members of her own community – especially certain older men who dominated claims to knowledge in the community – of trying to destroy their identity. After conflicts in the community, some of them in public, Sis Iboy abandoned her efforts, not because she was convinced by evidence that her ideas were false, but because her view was disliked by those in authority. In a discourse of 'soldiers' seeking to defend a position, not of 'scouts' seeking evidence and self-correction, a young, creative, evidence-focused woman yields to the arbitrary authority of more powerful political actors. Put yourself in her position. A relatively powerless individual in a relatively powerless group would see little payoff in resisting pressure from community authorities in a controversy around cultural identity and political direction.

The philosopher Paul Boghossian opens his book *Fear of Knowledge* with competing views of how humans came to live in the Americas.[11] Professional archaeologists say that people entered the Americas by crossing the Bering Strait from Siberia some 10,000 years ago. This belief is supported by archaeological findings and DNA evidence. By contrast, some representatives of Native American groups say that people were created in situ by mythological creative powers of ancestors. Sebastian LeBeau, an official of the Cheyenne River Sioux, stated: 'We know where we came from. We are the descendants of the Buffalo people. They came from inside the earth after supernatural spirits prepared this world for humankind to live here.'[12]

If our criterion for determining truth was to draw on evidence that is independent from people's beliefs or from the authority of any individual, then only the migration theory has a chance of being true (while always subject to revision in light of new evidence). Yet in cases like this one, and in Sis Iboy's story, some scholars have been willing to dismiss the need for evidence entirely, and instead defer to cultural authority. Many say that different claims can be 'equally valid', implying that we should not dispute their claims to truth, even when these clearly contradict each other.[13] So, there is a dilemma. The professed Sioux belief ties the people to the land, and in turn gives them a claim to that land, one which may even stand up in court. We may want the Sioux to have land and self-determination. We may not want to denigrate their beliefs. So we may be willing to let the story stand, unchallenged, because we feel it shows respect to do so, and because it helps an outcome we support.

But uncritically accepting fantastical claims is the wrong way to go. If a group deserves rights over land that their ancestors have long claimed, then that should be achieved without having to say that fictions are facts, based on the cultural authority of those who make the claims. Why? Because it opens the door to abuse and tyranny.

Among the most egregious examples of injustice grounded in the assertion of supernatural belief from authority are the punitive uses of claims to witchcraft (see Figure 2.1). Renaissance Italy gives us the example of Chiara Signorini, a peasant woman of Modena.[14] The landowner on whose fields she lived fell ill, and Signorini was accused of causing the illness by witchcraft. It so happened that the accusation followed a land dispute between Signorini and the landowner. Signorini was interrogated, tortured, found guilty and sentenced to lifelong servitude. That verdict was reached not because the claim of witchcraft was true (it wasn't), or because plausible evidence was given (it wasn't), but because the claimant had political power. The same scenario has played out, and still plays out today, in countries the world over. In the 21st century there is still a need for organizations such as the International Alliance to End Witch Hunts[15] and the Witchcraft and Human Rights Information

Figure 2.1: Illustrations from John Ashton's *The Devil in Britain and America* (1896), purporting to show women engaged in witchcraft: having commerce with a devil (left) and brewing a witches' broth (right)

Network.[16] That is why, in response to that sociology professor who chided me for doubting the supernatural claims of a community, we *must* demand evidence for claims to knowledge, especially when those claims are extraordinary and especially when there is pressure to grant them from arbitrary authority.

The problem is that humans are especially susceptible to the soldier mindset. We like to defend a position more than we like to dispassionately seek out the facts. Our sense of group identity and social allegiance can be stronger than the value we place on truth. When we think we are looking for the truth we are often just shopping for justifications, looking for reasons to support the things we already believe and to ignore those we don't.

When we have decided in advance what action we want to take, then the truth may no longer be relevant. That is, not until the consequences of our ill-justified actions hit us in the face. But that approach has things exactly the wrong way around. We must first find out what is true and then let those facts be our reasons for action. That is why soldiers need scouts if they are going to live to fight another day.

3
THE TWO REALITIES

> There are two realities – physical reality and social
> reality – in which truth may be at issue. The two should be
> aligned, but in the final analysis, one (physical reality) is
> more important than the other.

Suppose you are searched by immigration officials who find a pistol in your briefcase. You provide documents showing that you are authorized to carry the firearm. You are escorted by a stern official to a windowless room in the bowels of the facility. Now, two matters are at issue. One: Is it true that there was a pistol in the case? Two: Are you legally authorized to carry it?

The question of whether there was a pistol in your briefcase is a matter of *physical reality* or brute reality. It was either there or it wasn't. As we saw in Chapter 1, there may be some wiggle-room, as we do need to agree on what the English word *pistol* refers to (or *firearm*, or whatever word appears in the relevant legal code). To solve this, we can always triangulate by asking the question using different words: *pistol*, *gun*, *weapon*, and so on. But nothing we can say would change the fact that the physical object was in the case.

The question of whether you are authorized to carry the gun is a matter of *social reality*. Authority to carry a gun is defined by legal rights and duties. Rights and duties are not created by physical matter but by social agreement. So, your rights can be revoked and changed solely by changes in collective agreement. For example, if gun laws change, your licence card may no longer be valid, though nothing about the card or the gun has physically changed.

An anecdote illustrates the fundamental distinction between physical and social reality. I once had a new bicycle and rode it to town. I locked it outside a shopping centre, and when I returned I found that someone had locked it in place using a second heavy-duty lock. Two things were true. (1) The bicycle belonged to me. (2) I couldn't remove it. The fact that I could not remove it was a brute fact. It was simply not a physical possibility (I did not have appropriate tools). What made this true was something causal about the physical world, something that had no relation to my beliefs about the bike. By contrast, the fact that the bicycle belonged to me was a social fact. What made that true was not a fact about the bicycle, but a fact about how people treated that bicycle.

My predicament was soon explained. A woman came marching up with a police officer in tow. Her bike had recently been stolen and this was it, she said. No, I said, I recently bought it new. The matter was settled when I produced legal documentation of the purchase. That documentation had its power by virtue of binding statements made by people, using language. My valid purchase of the bike gave me certain rights and duties; for example, the right to ride the bicycle where and when I want, the right to sell it, the duty to obey traffic rules, and so on. Those rights and duties are social realities but they were never far from nature's cannons. In this case, those cannons are not the social rules of property rights but the police officer's physical instruments of force. Had I not been able to produce proof of my rights over the bike in social reality, I might have been deprived of my rights in physical reality.

The distinction between facts in physical reality and facts in social reality is everywhere. Suppose you have a one-kilogram lump of nickel. The statement 'This weighs one kilogram' is true in physical reality while 'This is worth $16' is true in social reality. Or 'The cricket ball hit the batter's stumps' (true in physical reality) versus 'The batter is out' (true in social reality). Or 'They were holding hands' (physical reality) versus 'They are a couple' (social reality). In each case, the first statement is a physical fact. It can't be changed by beliefs or attitudes.

Facts about social reality are true because of human actions, statements called 'status function declarations', to use philosopher John Searle's term.[1] These declarations change the status of things. They include contracts of sale, awards, registrations, convictions, rulings, promises, and much more. But status function declarations are limited in that they can never create or change matters of *physical* reality. Just because the Nuer people of the Sudan explained to the anthropologist E.E. Evans-Pritchard that 'twins are birds',[2] that statement did not make the claim true in any literal sense. Similarly, just because the congregation at St Patrick's Cathedral might say that the bread taken at Holy Communion is actually the body of Christ does not make it so (see Figure 3.1).

Figure 3.1: The Eucharist – a priest elevates the host during mass

THE TWO REALITIES

The two realities must not be confused. But they should be aligned. For example, being licensed to drive (a fact in social reality) should correlate with being capable of operating a motor vehicle safely (a fact in physical reality). These can be dangerously delinked, for example when an elderly driver retains their licence yet is no longer able to drive safely, or in a corrupt nation where you can buy a driver's licence on the black market, whether or not you know how to drive.

While physical reality and social reality are different in kind, truth matters in both domains. But the two realms should be kept distinct if we are to use truth to our advantage. Here is the most important reason why. Some people hold the view that truth is relative, malleable and socially constructed. This is correct *only* in the domain of *social* reality. It is true that values, rules, rights and duties are created by agreement among people. These things are true precisely because we collectively agree that they are true. But the same does not apply in physical reality. Under the right circumstances, the words 'I pronounce you man and wife' actually make it true that you are man and wife. But under no circumstances do the words 'I pronounce you safe from bullets' make you safe from bullets.

Political power lies in the relationship between the two realities. It is in this sense that war is the final argument of kings, why governments have what the sociologist Max Weber called a 'monopoly of the legitimate use of physical force',[3] or what is often called a monopoly on violence. Laws exist in the realm of social reality. But they are backed up, ultimately, only by the incontrovertible, uncancellable forces of physical reality: ultimately, imprisonment or even execution. Behind every rule and regulation in social reality is a long and winding corridor that leads to a prison cell. This may sound extreme, but consider what happens when you refuse to pay a speeding fine. You will be asked, then reminded, then cautioned, then visited, and finally, physically detained. In the competition between the two realities, brute reality always wins.

But we don't want to lose sight of the social power of shared fictions. While false beliefs are bad reasons for action, they can be useful as indirect signals for social cohesion. Recall our earlier discussion (Chapter 2) of supernatural beliefs. What's the good of these outlandish claims? There is a phenomenon called collective deception, as the anthropologist Chris Knight and colleagues have termed it.[4] In many cultures, it is important to state your adherence to certain beliefs in order to signal that you belong to the group. This is easy to see in large, formalized religions. The first pillar of Islam, known as Shahadah, is the profession of faith: 'There is no God but God, and Muhammad is the Messenger of God.' Stating an article of faith is like wearing the colours of a sport team. It makes a public commitment that you support just that team, against all others.

The signalling function of unverifiable beliefs is also a feature of small cultural communities. For example, members of the Indigenous community of Kri-speaking people with whom I work in upland Laos profess beliefs in various supernatural entities that are active in their houses, villages and natural landscapes. The Kri say that these entities have supernatural powers to affect weather, health and fortune. Whether they sincerely believe these claims or not, the claims are a statement of faith that advertises their commitment to being a member of their group, and draws a clear line between them and outsiders.

Using statements of belief in these ways, groups of people tacitly agree to act as if certain statements were true, but where, importantly, the truth of those statements cannot be shown. Indeed, the statements are highly unlikely to be true. Creationists say that all life on earth was consciously designed and created by a divine being in a matter of days. Middle-class Laotians say that having a new motorcar blessed by monks will reduce the risk of car accidents, and that having tattoos applied by monks with special powers can protect your body from bullets. The Dorze people of southern Ethiopia say that the local leopards are devout Christians. These statements need not be analysed as real truth claims, in the scientific sense that they yield predictions that are not falsified by evidence, or even in the everyday sense that they give us sound reasons for action. Anthropologist Dan Sperber has analysed such beliefs as social symbolism.[5] What does this mean?

Symbolic belief should not be mistaken for true belief. It is tempting to think that the Lao people who have their cars blessed by monks for safety reasons are deluded. But do they really think that they are safer in traffic because of the monks' blessings? Granted, there may be an element of Pascal's Wager: If the belief turns out to be false, the cost of having the ritual done was only a minor loss, but if true, the ritual could be a life-saver. But that is not what the practice is about. The blessing ritual is a public affair. When monks visit you and perform the rituals, people in the village see. And the monks leave garlands and inscriptions in the car, which are not to be removed. These advertise your commitment to local conventions.

This is the signalling function of stated belief. What matters is not that you believe, but that people hear you say that you believe. At the same time, the belief is a fiction, and therefore a poor reason for action. Monks' blessings won't save you from a crash if you are driving recklessly. But these acted-upon beliefs still need to be taken seriously because their effects are real. It's just that they aren't real in the way they say. We can see this because people who have monks bless their cars don't put their trust entirely in that mechanism. They still do all the other things people do to lower the risks of coming to harm. They wear seat belts, they have their cars serviced, they change the brake pads when needed, and so on. Does this mean that their words are empty?

There is an important sense in which symbolic/fantastical beliefs may have positive functions, if taken seriously but not literally. Such beliefs may serve to raise people's awareness of dangers that deserve attention (such as risks of harm from traffic accidents), or they may convey 'deeper truths' as in allegories. Most stories, from myths to novels to movies, are about two things: (1) what the story is about, and (2) what the story is really about. George Orwell's novella *Animal Farm* is 'about' a bunch of farm animals who stage a revolution against their human owner but find that their utopian society fails. It is 'really about' the dynamics of power, the corruption of revolutionary ideals and the dangers of totalitarian regimes. We are not meant to believe that the specific events related are true – that there really was a boar named Old Major who really did inspire an animal rebellion on an English farm, and so on – but Orwell certainly wants us to accept the thinly veiled critique of the historical figures Karl Marx and Vladimir Lenin who inspired the Old Major character.

The philosopher Ludwig Wittgenstein showed that words can be used in different 'language games', that is, different kinds of activity using language (compare, say, sports commentary versus joke-telling versus gossip).[6] Each game implies its own set of rules. Consider the statement made by a friend of mine in Laos that certain monks can tattoo you with ancient inscriptions that will protect you from harm. The tattoos can stop bullets, he says. Does my friend really believe that these claims are true? I don't think so, at least not in the same way he believes that a bullet to the head will kill you. This can be proven by asking a person with such a tattoo if he will agree for you to pull out a gun and fire it at him. After all, he said the tattoo would stop bullets. My friend says, 'No, that's not how it works.' He knows he would not be safe from a bullet, tattoo or no tattoo. So, when he says that tattoos stop bullets, he is not playing the reality game. He is playing the signalling game.[7]

It is important not to get these games mixed up. Remember the sociology professor who chided me for questioning the epistemology of other cultures. The professor's challenge implies that we shouldn't dismiss cultural beliefs, especially when they come from cultures different than our own. But this doctrine mixes the signalling game with the reality game. It is shallow and dangerous.

It is shallow because it treats claims uncritically. The two claims – (1) that if you shoot me, I will be injured, and (2) that if you shoot me, I will be unharmed because I have this tattoo – are different kinds of claim. To say that my friend's belief that tattoos will stop bullets is just as valid as my belief that they will not is to treat my friend as a fool. He is not. In the reality game, he knows what bullets will do.

The doctrine of equal validity is dangerous because it does not distinguish between the two kinds of beliefs we have been discussing so far in this chapter. We can call them actionable beliefs and signalling beliefs (see Chapter 4). Failing to make that distinction can cause real harms, through kinds of collateral damage we discuss further in Chapter 4.

People are often accepting of outlandish claims when those claims are found in other cultures. Some feel that other people are authorities over their own cultures. But that goes against the foundational insight, attributed to principles developed during the Enlightenment, that no personal authority is sacred, not even the word of

God. That is, we should not believe something is true purely because someone with authority says so. What is needed is evidence. Of course, experts will likely know better what that evidence might be, and so we should cultivate respect for that knowledge.[8] But if we accept something as true, it should be on the evidence that expert provides, not simply on their say-so. Physicist David Deutsch writes: 'Knowledge exists. But nothing can authorise it.'[9] Recall the case of Chiara Signorini, accused of causing her landowner's illness through witchcraft. Should Chiara – or any of the thousands of people accused of witchcraft today – yield to the claim from authority that the accusations are true? Surely not. So, why should you accept similar claims that happen not to threaten your personal well-being, such as my friend's idea that gifted monks have supernatural powers. If the doctrine of equal validity cannot be applied consistently, then we ought to invoke the old principle *Quod gratis asseritur, gratis negatur*. What can be asserted freely – that is, without evidence – can be equally freely dismissed. Authority is not evidence.

As we have seen, some people regard it as ethical to accept unevidenced statements when they like what those statements lead to. For example, Indigenous assertions of supernatural connection with land have been admitted as evidence in land claims. In a 2024 US Congress Oversight Hearing on 'Examining the Opportunities and Challenges of Land Consolidation in Indian Country', Chairman Ryman LeBeau of the Cheyenne River Sioux gave a statement pleading for improved land title arrangements. While LeBeau's statement focuses mostly on livelihoods and economic issues, its opening page includes the following:[10]

> In our belief, Tunkasila, Wakan Tanka, Grandfather, the Creator gave the first woman and first man the breath of life at Wind Cave in the Black Hills. Together with life, Tunkasila blessed us with liberty and a sacred duty to care for Unci Maka, Grandmother Earth. Ours is the original land of our Lakota Oyate, prior to America.

In Indigenous land claims around the world, statements like these are made to support a group's claim to have a special connection to land, which in turn supports their rights to occupy and control that land. Suppose we agree on two things. One, the Cheyenne River Sioux should be granted the rights that they seek over their ancestral lands. Two, the creation story is fiction, and no evidence could show that a supernatural creator breathed life into the first man and woman. How do we reconcile these two things? The answer is by not treating claims of supernatural belief as literal truth claims. Ryman LeBeau is signalling as much with his opening phrase, 'In our belief'. You can acknowledge the importance of the creation story, of what it tells us about the relation between a community and their land, and about the transmission of ideas across generations, without having to say that it's literally true. Recall our earlier remark in this chapter that every story is about two things: what it's about and what it's really about.

But the power of stories cuts both ways. Supernatural beliefs can be invoked to empower the disenfranchised, but they can also be exploited at their cost. Consider a case of Indigenous land rights in relation to the billion-dollar Nam Theun 2 hydroelectricity project, one of the biggest infrastructure projects in Laos. When it was nearing completion in 2007, officials hit a snag. A small village of Indigenous people from the Ahoe ethnic group was situated in the flood zone just upstream from the new dam wall. Before the dam could be impounded, flooding the plateau and creating the reservoir for power-generation, the Ahoe people would have to vacate their traditional village area and be relocated to new lands. But they refused. The Ahoe elderly matriarch and spiritual leader, Mrs Khamsone (see Figure 3.2), insisted that the guardian spirits of their village lands were unwilling to relocate, and that

Figure 3.2: Matriarch of Ahoe ethnicity, Mrs Khamsone, left, at her home in Sop Hia Village, Central Laos

forced removal would upset these spirits and bring illness, misfortune and death upon her people.

For a while, there was a stand-off. Authorities from the World Bank and Électricité de France were paralysed. They had signed complex legal agreements that protected the rights of ethnic communities. This small community of hunter-gatherers was blocking a billion-dollar programme at the final step before commercial operations could begin. Bank and company officials had no idea what to do. That's when a local Lao official saw the obvious. He understood the logic of local spirits. Just as Mrs Khamsone could invoke the belief that spirits are dangerous when disturbed, the Lao official could invoke the belief that spirits can be placated by ritual sacrifice. He simply asked the power company to pay for a buffalo sacrifice, as an offering to those spirits, to ensure they would not be angry. The ritual took place, the spirits were placated, the village was relocated, and the dam was impounded, flooding Ahoe lands forever.

The power company had dodged a bullet. The solution was easier than they could have imagined: a few hundred dollars for a buffalo sacrifice and a public ritual. In a twist that ruthlessly exploited the escape-hatch of cultural authority, power company officials took the supernatural beliefs that had created the problem and turned them to their advantage.

Mrs Khamsone was surely correct that forced relocation onto unfamiliar lands, heavily populated by more dominant ethnic groups, would harm her people. But the causes of those harms would not be spirit anger. Ahoe people's fears of negative consequences of relocation would be realized by societal and physiological mechanisms that are well understood. When social cohesion is altered, people lose their support networks. When established livelihoods are removed and new ones provided, people go to the bottom of the social ladder. When people experience anxiety and stress of upheaval, health impacts follow. But by claiming that the harms would be caused by displeased spirits, the effect was to divert attention away from the real causes. This made it possible for power company officials to cheaply display their acceptance of local beliefs and norms and get what they wanted anyway, without actually addressing the underlying problems. As we noted in the last chapter, if a cause is just, we should not have to subscribe to fictions to make the case.

There are two realities: social reality and physical reality. But social reality is secondary, contingent and tenuous. All power ultimately comes down to control over natural causes, even if social reality plays a role, for example, in legitimizing one party's use of force. In social reality, a bar of gold can make you rich, but in brute reality it is merely a paperweight. Some suggest that *all* truth is *social*. This idea is either trivial (because we need words to talk) or false (because pain always hurts). But more importantly, the claim that all reality is socially constructed is the height of arrogance. To imagine that human interpretations have any effect on nature's cannons is to believe in magic. When you are incarcerated, no amount of belief or meditation will allow you to pass through walls. It is precisely and ultimately only those natural forces that are marshalled in the exercising of human power. The principle of *Ultima ratio regum* – the final argument of kings – means that warring nations will never agree to resolve their disputes with a coin toss. Social reality always gives way to the forces of nature: *Ultima ratio naturae*.

4
COLLATERAL EFFECTS

> All statements give off information about the social identity
> of the person making them. People often use statements
> for purely signalling purposes, with no regard for truth,
> creating a form of collateral damage that is as old as
> language itself.

What if I told you the moon landings were faked? The statement gives you information on two levels. On one level, it is about the moon landings. On its face, the statement makes a claim that can be tested for its truth value. On another level, it tells you something about me. It lets you in on what kind of a person I am, and what other things I might say. If you meet someone who says that the landings were faked, you could make better-than-chance predictions about other things they might believe: their thoughts on assassinations, UFO visits, terrorist attacks, current political candidates, and more. Deep down, few of us really have hard evidence that the moon landings *weren't* faked. But most of us accept the ample evidence that men walked on the moon, and we reject alternatives that are highly unlikely. Someone who doubts what is well-evidenced may be doing so primarily to signal a broader message: that you should be sceptical, that you shouldn't trust the authority of the state, or that you shouldn't be a sheep. And so for some people, it doesn't matter whether the landings were faked or not. *Saying* that they were faked sends a message. If that message happens to pollute the informational environment with a falsehood, well, that's just collateral damage: the friendly fire of the infosphere.

The principle of signalling one's identity by the claims one makes doesn't just risk causing an increase in the frequency of false or unprovable statements. It can also *incentivize* people to make false or unprovable statements. To demonstrate the dangers of this, let us dive more deeply into a phenomenon we encountered in the last chapter: belief in the supernatural, ghosts and magic, sorcerers and spirits.

People everywhere profess beliefs in supernatural entities. The reasons for this are many, but we focus here on one. Outlandish claims help forge group cohesion. When people commit to statements that are both far-fetched and unprovable (for example, that the dead live on in another world), the surprising and counterintuitive nature of the claims has a socially binding effect.

Millions believe that Jesus Christ rose from the dead 2,000 years ago and that He is here with us today. The claim that someone can rise from the dead runs deeply counter to our everyday experience. We have all lost loved ones, whether it may be grandparents, parents, siblings, friends, or even our own children. And we have had the experience that nothing we do or say can bring those loved ones back. We may feel that they are looking over our shoulder or that some connection continues. We may even imagine ourselves consulting them when we need advice. But in a real and deep sense, we know that they are gone, permanently and irrevocably.

Why would the death of Jesus Christ be any different? It is different because the claim is not really about truth. Those who say Christ died for our sins, or that He rose from the dead, are playing a different language game. They are not saying these things to inform or update people on actionable intelligence, as a military scout might do. (Or if they are, the message they want to send is not encoded in the literal meaning of their words, as with Orwell's *Animal Farm*.) They are saying something about themselves. And they are enacting social bonds, using the mechanism of assertion to signal their commitment to a social group, the group who believe that thing.

The identity game with language works better when the signalling belief is hard to prove – and indeed, hard to believe. Why aren't there religious commitments that are obvious and easily proven? Why do no religions commit publicly to claims that feathers are lighter than rocks, that sunshine is warm, or that what goes up must come down? Because nobody would dispute these claims and so committing to them does not help distinguish between insiders and outsiders. When you commit to a belief that is not just hard to prove but also unlikely to be true, you are sticking your neck out. You are showing that you are prepared to be called a fool (by the other tribe or religion) but you are publicly committing anyway. These beliefs exploit language for the purpose of creating sides, not for the purpose of improving knowledge.[1]

Here is how unevidenced outlandish beliefs create social bonds. It is not enough to simply state the beliefs. We must act, at least part of the time, as if we really believed them. This might seem dismissive of heartfelt beliefs, but it is clear that when someone 'believes' something, this can mean more than one thing. Some beliefs are *actionable beliefs*. These beliefs are never switched off. Solid objects cannot go through walls. Liquid spreads when spilled. The higher the fall, the harder you hit the ground. Because I have actionable beliefs about gravity and the motion of solid objects, I take the stairs when I want to get from the top floor of the building to the ground, even though jumping from the window would be quicker. We never have time out from abiding by these actionable beliefs. On the other hand, there are *signalling beliefs*. I may state such beliefs, and sometimes I may act as if I believe them. But unlike actionable beliefs, I can, and often do, abandon them at will.

I mentioned this earlier in relation to tattoos that are said to stop bullets. People say that it's true, yet they will duck for cover in a shootout. This is the difference between a magical tattoo and a suit of military body armour. Your beliefs about the efficacy of the body armour are actionable beliefs, unlike your beliefs about the tattoo. This is the difference between assertions as reasons for action and assertions as acts of identity. When push comes to shove, you will drop the signalling belief or risk bad consequences.

We have argued in this book that truth is for striving at, for the collective good. Modern science is built on this premise. The foundation of a scientific outlook is the idea that nothing is exempt from being criticized, and if necessary, updated. On this view, finding out that you are wrong is a victory. It means ridding yourself of a fiction and getting one step closer to truth. And it contains a paradox. It is a commitment to the revocability of all commitments.

Crucial early steps in developing the scientific outlook had to do with health. In the ancient world, Hippocrates revolutionized the conception of health and sickness.[2] Before his time, the dominant belief was that medical conditions were caused by supernatural powers and processes. Accordingly, many treatments for illness involved prayer and ritual. But because those beliefs were fictional, treatments had limited effect on ameliorating sickness or preventing suffering and premature death.

Imagine you are living in Ancient Greece and your newborn daughter develops a septal defect, the congenital condition known as a hole in the heart. This means that there is an opening between chambers of her heart that shouldn't be there.[3] This causes problems by changing her blood oxygen content or increasing the amount of blood going through her lungs. But of course, you cannot see into her heart. You only see the symptoms. She is often short of breath. Her legs and feet are swelling. Her heartbeat is irregular. But you have no idea of the true cause. All you can do is pray. As she grows, you watch your daughter's condition worsen. You once assumed that she would one day see you die from old age. Instead, you witness her early death, after a childhood with debilitating pulmonary hypertension (high blood pressure in the lung arteries). You bury her, not knowing what killed her. You blame malevolent supernatural forces.

Hippocrates and his associates and students started a tradition that would ultimately make it possible to treat a septal defect in the first few months of life and allow a child to live a normal, long and healthy life. They revolutionized medicine by treating illness as a domain of actionable beliefs. They wanted to find physical causes for illness. This meant collecting data, comparing cases, testing hypotheses and updating them. It meant fostering a scientific mindset.[4] This mindset combines *creativity* with *criticism*. Creativity means thinking outside the box, looking for new ideas that might lead to solutions we're not seeing. Criticism means subjecting those creative ideas to rigorous testing, trying to shoot them down, and if necessary discarding or correcting them.

It is no accident that the field of medicine is where some of the earliest foundations of science were laid. With medicine, we all have skin in the game. Nothing says drop your superstitions like the prospect of a dead child. Thanks to Hippocrates, and his intellectual descendants, we can now prevent thousands of illnesses and millions of early deaths.

But freedom from dogma has a price. That price is eternal vigilance. The signalling power of outlandish beliefs constantly threatens to overwhelm the quest for truth. Extraordinarily, while the culture of medical science has persisted for millennia, lowering human suffering and extending our lives, people who reject medical science have never gone away. An example is those who believe in the healing power of prayer. For many people, prayer makes sense when you don't know what to do. It can make you feel like you are taking some action when you would otherwise be paralysed. It can reassure people. But confusing it with an actionable belief is not just a route to tragedy and disaster, it is a crime.

The Followers of Christ are a US-based Christian sect. They say that prayer can treat the ill and that it should be used in place of modern medicine.[5] If that assertion were sequestered to the realm of signalling beliefs and not really acted upon – like the bullet-stopping tattoo – this might be harmless. The problem arises when it crosses the line and is taken up as a reason for real-world action.

Mariah Walton was born in the 1990s and raised in Idaho as one of ten children. Her parents were members of the Followers of Christ. Mariah was born with a septal defect. Instead of carrying out the now-routine PFO Closure procedure to mend the hole in her heart and give her a normal, healthy life, her parents attributed the condition to evil spirits and refused medical help. Instead, they prayed. They chose to do what the Ancient Greeks had no alternative other than to do. They let their daughter's health deteriorate. As a result, Mariah Walton became permanently disabled by pulmonary hypertension. Mariah has campaigned to change Idaho's legal protections of child abuse and neglect by religious groups, seeking to have her parents prosecuted.

Another victim of the Followers of Christ is Brian Hoyt. He crushed two bones in his ankle in a wrestling tryout at the age of 12. The injury was left untreated. Brian was abused by family members, he says, 'because I didn't have enough faith to let God come in and heal me'. When the school forced Brian's mother to take him to a doctor, Brian was given a cast and medicines. But when he got home, his family threw away the medicines and removed the cast.

Idaho State Senator Lee Heider was among the lawmakers who had the power to intervene, in the interests of those children's welfare. A bill came before the Idaho state government to make it possible to prosecute families who failed to protect children like Mariah Walton and Brian Hoyt from harm. Neighbouring Oregon had made the change to remove special protections based on religious belief, and there had been several successful prosecutions for criminal mistreatment, negligent homicide and second-degree manslaughter for child deaths in Followers of Christ families. But Senator Heider chose instead to protect those who had neglected and abused children like

Walton and Hoyt. He defended the practices as 'faith healing' and argued that the government should not intervene, on religious grounds and the First Amendment. When pressed on the fact 'that children are dying unnecessarily' as a result of exemptions, Heider said this: 'Are we going to stop Methodists from reading the New Testament? Are we going to stop Catholics receiving the sacraments? That's what these people believe in. They spoke to me and pointed to a tremendous number of examples where Christ healed people in the New Testament.'

Heider is confusing signalling beliefs for actionable beliefs. He is confusing what those stories are about with what they are really about. The result is that children's lives are mere collateral damage. Heider's comments show that he regards the withholding of medical treatment from living, breathing, suffering children as equivalent to everyday identity-marking practices like the retelling of fantastic stories from sacred books and associated performative rituals. Storytelling and ritual can have positive functions. And they do not normally cause direct physical harms. But that cannot be said about the choice to withhold medical treatment from children based on a fictitious belief. When signalling beliefs are treated as actionable beliefs, this brings out the worst in us. This confusion is at the root of our greatest evils, from child abuse to all-out war, waged in the name of social identity. These forms of collateral damage are unforgivable.

Communities such as the Followers of Christ, and many like them around the world and throughout history, perpetrate collateral damage by choosing to take signalling beliefs literally. The heinous nature of that avoidable damage is especially stark when it comes to children. If you want to be jolted into seeing how far we've come in medical treatments over the last century in particular, you can visit any 19th-century church graveyard and see the tombstones of the infants who died from conditions that are now entirely preventable, thanks to steady progress in the tradition of Hippocrates. In the cemeteries of the Followers of Christ today, the picture is no different. In 2016, well into the 21st century, the sect's cemetery in Peaceful Valley, Idaho, was 'full of graves marking the deaths of children who lived a day, a week, a month' (see Figure 4.1).[6]

Figure 4.1: 'The Followers of Christ's cemetery is full of graves marking the deaths of children who lived a day, a week, a month'

COLLATERAL EFFECTS

When I look at an infant's gravestone, I cannot imagine a more potent illustration of the adage that 'all evil is due to insufficient knowledge'.[7] Recall that this remark is less about evil than it is about the principle of optimism. It means that the more we know, the better things can be. If we do not try to find new knowledge and correct our own beliefs, the world does not get better. And this is only possible if we strive for that new knowledge, which can only be done in a culture that fosters pride in proving ourselves wrong and revising our beliefs.

Making the world better is what truth is for. Yet the evils deriving from lack of knowledge persist. Albinism is a genetic condition that causes lack of pigmentation in the eyes, hair and skin. It is a result of mutations in genes that encode for proteins which synthesize or transport melanin. Melanin gives skin its colour and shields it from the harms of ultraviolet radiation. In the realm of physical reality, albinism brings harms such as high rates of skin cancer, along with other pathologies associated with the genetic condition. Globally, albinism affects about one in 20,000 people. But in certain areas albinism is far more frequent. In parts of sub-Saharan Africa, more than one in 1,500 people have albinism (see Figure 4.2).

In these areas, false beliefs about albinism cross the line from superstition to action, with tragic results. These beliefs cast people with albinism as malevolent, contagious, defective and magical. Here is what a 2011 study had to say about the persecution of people with albinism in the Great Lakes region of central east Africa:[8]

WHAT IS TRUTH FOR?

[T]he atrocities committed against albinos have received widespread attention because of various crimes reported, such as infanticide, kidnapping, amputations, and decapitations, committed for purposes of supplying highly valued body parts used for amulets, which are then sold in underground witchcraft markets. For example, up to $75,000 may be offered for a set of arms, legs, ears, and genitals from an individual with albinism. Thus, albinos must live in a constant state of guilt and angst, often forced to flee their homes and live in solitude to avoid the albino hunters.

Figure 4.2: Isaac Mwaura with Bianca Chacha and Gabriel Kinyanjui

Isaac Mwaura, a member of Kenya's Parliament and national coordinator for the Albinism Society of Kenya, speaks to Bianca Chacha and Gabriel Kinyanjui at their home in 2015. Mwaura took in both children after they survived abduction attempts.

Imagine it. You are an object of fear and disgust and are hunted for your body parts, all because of a simple genetic disorder. In cases like these, facts don't matter. What matters is that a group is bonded by a common belief and a common reason for action. Again, the more outlandish the belief, the tighter it binds people together.

I have emphasized the dangers of confusing signalling beliefs with actionable beliefs. And I suggested that signalling beliefs may be harmless as long as they aren't used as reasons for action, as with faith healers and albino hunters. But there is a view that no falsehoods are harmless and that we should never subscribe to fictions, as a matter of principle. One reason for this is that these beliefs have less obvious harms, which we don't always see. These are the higher-level harms of being uncritical, especially when this promotes the acceptance of beliefs that come to us from authorities we cannot question.

Czech statesman Václav Havel gives the case of a grocer in the former Eastern Bloc who puts a sign in his window saying 'Workers of the world, unite'.[9] This slogan carries a wholesome message, but in this context it is a signal of compliance with the regime. Not posting the sign would itself be a sign, an implication that the shop owner is not on board with the programme. So, the slogan is no longer about the *content* of the message but rather about what the message signals about its sender. The result is that the grocer primarily signals not his support of regime's sentiment but his submission to it. Havel writes:

> Individuals need not believe all these mystifications, but they must behave as though they did, or they must at least tolerate them in silence, or get along well with those who work with them. For this reason, however, they must live within a lie. They need not accept the lie. It is enough for them to have accepted their life with it and in it. For by this very fact, individuals confirm the system, fulfill the system, make the system, are the system.

When you overtly make statements that express majority beliefs, you contribute to making those beliefs dominant in a society. The expressed beliefs may well be true, and good, but expressing just those beliefs and not others has the effect of suppressing the diversity of ideas circulating in your social network. It lowers the chances that dominant ideas will be challenged, removing a crucial mechanism for improving ideas through error-correction.

In Havel's example, the issue is not whether workers of the world should unite. The problem is this. When a statement is used as an identity signal, this de-links (1) the reason for making the assertion from (2) the truth or wisdom of the assertion. That is, it turns the statement into what the philosopher Harry Frankfurt has technically defined as bullshit: a statement made by someone who is not really interested in whether it is true or not.[10] Once that de-linking occurs, the content of the assertion can drift away from any mooring in reality. If there turn out to be problems with the assertion, it becomes harder and harder to challenge.

Furthermore, it becomes possible for a majority of people to no longer believe the statement and yet still *say* they do. This is what political scientist Timur Kuran calls *preference falsification*: expressing a publicly sanctioned view even though privately one believes otherwise.[11] The result can be a situation in which the majority of a population does not subscribe to a sanctioned view, yet that view continues to dominate the idea economy. The less a claim is publicly challenged, the more impervious it becomes, and the more useful it may be for those who have power and wish to abuse it.

Recall, again, Chiara Signorini, imprisoned for the false accusation of witchcraft. Her conviction was an arbitrary abuse of power, made on authority in the name of a fiction. Some argue that witchcraft accusations can be a positive mechanism of 'cultural healing' for dealing with local justice,[12] but such a mechanism is illiberal at best and promotes vigilantism at worst, where the stated reason for punishment ('you are a witch') is de-linked from any truthful reasons for wishing to exclude or punish a person. Thus, the accused receives no explanation, has no recourse, and there are no checks or balances on the justice system. Another way to frame witchcraft accusations as a positive force is that the scapegoating mechanism channels a group's aggression onto a single target as a way of avoiding the much-worse alternative, namely all-on-all violence.[13] But both of these justifications for using falsehoods for social control are unacceptable, for two reasons. One, they are susceptible to arbitrary abuse. Two, they are not open to objective appeal. If social functions like justice and prevention of violence are worth serving, they are worth serving well. So, if a person deserves to be ostracized for bad behaviour, then let people ostracize them for the real reason, not a fictitious one. And if violence should be reduced or prevented, do it without sacrificing a random community member.

The problem we have been exploring is the natural human tendency to put *tribe before truth*, to use philosopher Dan Kahan's phrase.[14] Saying that prayer alone can save a child puts tribe before truth. It is a bad reason for action. As we've seen, paradoxically this strengthens its power as a social signal, as it shows just how high a cost you are willing to pay for holding the belief. But the problem – as we learned from the Followers of Christ – is that *others* are often the ones who must pay the cost for our beliefs.

It is hard to overestimate the cruelty of fictitious beliefs when they cross into real life, whether this occurs in traditional or modern society, in the deep past or in today's world. An example is the modern conspiracy theory, which can bind online communities but also leak into the real world with awful results. Six-year-old Noah Pozner was among the 25 people killed in December 2012 by a man roaming through a Connecticut elementary school with an assault rifle. It is difficult to imagine what Noah's parents went through on that day. It is even harder to imagine their subsequent experience of being confronted – both online and in person – by people claiming that the shooting never happened, and that their son never existed.[15] The parents of Noah and other victims have set up organizations to counter these hoaxers, and to provide support for families in the face of denials of their grief.[16]

Did Noah Pozner die in a mass shooting at Sandy Hook in 2012, or was his story fabricated by state actors? The most radical form of relativism would allow that these positions are equally valid. But can you imagine anyone saying that the Sandy Hook parents and deniers have 'equally valid' perspectives on the events? We feel immediately that there is no comparison between the Noah Pozner case and the case of, say, the competing claims about origins of the Cheyenne River Sioux. One difference between the two cases concerns the politics of cultural authority. In the Cheyenne River Sioux case, we may want to allow that the community's claim is 'true for them' at the very least out of respect (while also allowing that the scientists' account may be 'true for them' too, given their evidence and arguments). Perhaps the competing claims could coexist. Allowing that the origin story is 'true' is a way to help legitimize a group's identity and cultural worldview, and to empower a disenfranchised community. But we are not really dealing here with alternative versions of the truth. They are claims of different kinds. Again, we have on the one hand a signalling belief, which serves its function whether it is true or not, and on the other hand an actionable belief, which is grounded in reality.

Is the dispute over Sandy Hook any different in kind? Or is it simply that we see no moral advantage to legitimizing the identity and worldview of a Sandy Hook denier? The consequences of such legitimization would be abhorrent. 'Conspiracy theorists erase the human aspect of history', said Noah's father Len Pozner. 'My child – who lived, who was a real person – is basically going to be erased.'[17] Similarly, though less heinously, magical origin stories also erase people, namely the real pioneers and ancestors whose epic true adventures would rival any supernatural fiction.

5
ALWAYS STRIVING, NEVER ARRIVING

While we can strive for truth, we can never arrive at it. If we become comfortable with this, we can achieve continual improvement through self-correction.

If we only try to confirm what we already think is true, we will easily succeed and trick ourselves into believing it. To get at the truth, we must instead try to disconfirm – or falsify – our beliefs. But this does not come naturally, as psychologist Peter Wason showed in his 1960 Rule Discovery Test.[1]

Imagine you are a participant in Wason's experiment. He has devised a rule that generates strings of numbers and your task is to figure out the rule. He writes the rule on a card which he places face down on the table. He tells you that 2-4-6 is allowed by the rule. Now you are invited to suggest as many strings of numbers as you like, and he will say 'Yes' if it fits his rule or 'No' if it doesn't. You tell him when you think you have the answer. You turn over the card to see if you are right.

Here is what happened. When told that 2-4-6 fits the rule, many participants first thought the rule must be 'Start with a number and keep adding 2'. So, they generated strings from that rule to ask if they fit. They would ask: What about 4-6-8? The experimenter would reply: Yes, that fits the rule. What about 6-8-10? Also yes. Okay, now, what about 22-24-26? Yes again. Then you announce you've got it. 'The rule is: Start with a number and keep adding 2.' But you're wrong.

The rule was actually this: 'Add any number bigger than the previous one.' All the sequences in the last paragraph fit this rule. If only you had tried to *disprove* your 'Keep adding 2' hypothesis, you would have quickly found this out. The key is to try to prove yourself wrong. Look for the vulnerability in your own belief. Check a string of numbers that would *not* follow from the rule you are imagining. If your hypothesis is 'keep adding 2' then you predict that 2-3-6 will get a 'no' answer. When you check this the answer surprises you. Yes, the experimenter says, the rule does allow the string 2-3-6. Your hunch was wrong. Hypothesis disconfirmed. Time to revise.

This is the essence of the scientific method.[2] When a scientist formulates an experiment, they start with a hypothesis: something they think might be true. The purpose of the experiment is to test that hypothesis. But the scientist cannot prove that the hypothesis is true. The scientist can only try – and perhaps fail – to disprove it. The approach is called falsification. It is the antidote to confirmation bias, the error in reasoning demonstrated in Wason's experiment. In theory, the scientist is like a military scout, focused on finding out the facts on the ground, so that sound decisions can be made. Like good scouts, good scientists want to know if they are wrong. They welcome challenges that may change their minds.

The true scientist is always striving but never arriving. But this doesn't quite fit the public ideal of 'settled science'. In the words of US politician Bernie Sanders: 'Science is science. There are no "alternative facts".'[3] I know what he wants to say, but the truth is that at the frontiers of scientific progress, claims to truth are contested, disputed and often corrected, only to be contested, disputed and corrected again. Science is never fully settled. Even when scientists are completely confident that they know the truth, they also know deep down that they may be wrong. The best they can hope for is to be able to say that they have tried, carefully and systematically, and in different ways, to disprove the thing they believe, and that they have so far failed to disprove it. And that no competing alternative has withstood the same rigorous testing. But being confident is not the same as being certain. It means that until further notice, what they believe has a high *probability* of being true.

Scientists might agree on certain facts while disagreeing on what those facts mean. Consider the example of the phenomenon known as Fast Radio Bursts, or FRBs. These are brief bursts of high frequency radio waves, most of which come from beyond our galaxy. The phenomenon was first discovered in 2007 by astrophysicists Duncan Lorimer and David Narkevic, who examined archival data supplied by the Parkes Observatory in Australia.[4] Many other FRBs have since been observed, and the observations themselves are not in dispute. Scientists can agree on the basic facts of an observation, such as their frequency, duration and direction of origin. The first-observed FRB 010724, known as the Lorimer Burst, lasted less than 5 milliseconds – five thousandths of a second – and originated some three degrees from the Small Magellanic Cloud.

But there is no agreement yet as to what causes these bursts, or what we should infer from them. They could be caused by collisions between dense objects such as black holes or neutron stars. They could be associated with the collapse of pulsars. They could even have something to do with extraterrestrial intelligence. Research continues, in the tradition of scientific progress. First, there is a puzzling observation. Then, a wave of follow-up research makes new findings and puts forward different explanations as each new piece of evidence comes to light. This is where we are currently at with FRBs. Next, hopefully, the new findings and analyses should converge, as scientists eliminate the incorrect ideas and take steps towards the truth.

Sometimes, of course, there are errors in the original observations, meaning that what were once considered facts turn out not to be facts at all. You have probably heard that spinach is especially high in iron content.

But legend has it that this belief comes from a scientist's error. Nineteenth-century German agricultural chemist Emil von Wolff is said to have misplaced a decimal point when measuring spinach's iron content. This meant that the recorded iron value was ten times higher than it should have been.

Other kinds of error can similarly lead us astray. Soon after the first FRBs were discovered, the plot thickened when a new observation further puzzled scientists. Looking for FRBs, they discovered similar signals but this time coming from earth. Known as *perytons*, these signals were 'millisecond-duration transients of terrestrial origin, whose frequency-swept emission mimics the dispersion of an astrophysical pulse that has propagated through tenuous cold plasma'.[5] For a time, the discovery 'cast a shadow over the interpretation of Fast Radio Bursts, which otherwise appear to be of extragalactic origin'. What was going on?

Astrophysicist Emily Petroff and her colleagues discovered the truth:

> Until now, the physical origin of the dispersion-mimicking perytons had remained a mystery. We have identified strong out-of-band emission at 2.3–2.5 GHz associated with several peryton events. Subsequent tests revealed that a peryton can be generated at 1.4 GHz when a microwave oven door is opened prematurely and the telescope is at an appropriate relative angle.

Yes, the perytons were occurring when workers at the Parkes Observatory facility were heating their lunch.

They would open the microwave door while the oven was still on, releasing a few-milliseconds burst of waves that would be recorded among the facility's archived observations.

Errors like these can of course be corrected and eradicated. But sometimes errors accumulate, especially when false beliefs enter the public imagination, or when claims of errors turn out themselves to be errors. Let us return to the story of spinach. In 1981, haematologist T.J. Hamblin wrote about the problem of fakes in science, starting with the idea that Popeye's superhuman strength came from eating spinach. The 19th-century discovery 'that spinach was as valuable a source of iron as red meat' turned out to be untrue, Hamblin wrote:[6]

> German chemists reinvestigating the iron content of spinach had shown in the 1930s that the original workers had put the decimal point in the wrong place and made a tenfold overestimate of its value. Spinach is no better for you than cabbage, Brussels sprouts, or broccoli. For a source of iron Popeye would have been better off chewing the cans.

Hamblin's account was a fun story, easy to remember and retell. It circulated for decades. But there was a problem. I referred earlier to the 'legend' of the misplaced decimal point. It is a legend because it never happened.

Thirty years after Hamblin's description of the misplaced decimal point, criminologist Mike Sutton did a deep historical dive into the myth of spinach and iron.[7] First, he found that Popeye never actually ate spinach for its iron content. A 1932 panel from the strip shows Popeye on all fours in a garden chomping on fresh spinach growing out of the ground (see Figure 5.1). His wife Olive Oyl looks on in alarm.

So it was Vitamin A and not iron after all. But to the science, second, Sutton found no evidence that the famous decimal-point error was ever made. Instead, as Sutton describes, an entirely different error occurred. In 1934, chemists from the University of Wisconsin analysed several plants for their iron content. Their study confused the measures of fresh and dried spinach. Dried spinach has a greater concentration of iron than fresh spinach, which led to a measurement error. The error was corrected in 1936. So, there was a grain of

Figure 5.1: Popeye, spinach advocate extraordinaire

truth after all in the story that a scientific error caused confusion about the iron content of spinach, but beyond that the story took on a life of its own.

The legend of the misplaced decimal point turned out to be fiction. So, we are not just dealing with a scientific myth. There is also a meta-myth. A myth about the myth. The myth is that spinach has ten times the iron content of other garden greens. The meta-myth is that this mistaken belief was caused by someone putting a decimal point in the wrong place. Both myths were picked up and repeated, decade after decade, without anyone ever checking the facts.

The spinach-iron case is a good cautionary tale because it illustrates how well fictions can stick in the public imagination and circulate quite independently of their origin. As Sutton concluded, it is 'a most embarrassing double irony' that so many writers cite the spinach-iron story 'with absolute confidence as a genuine example of the importance of checking facts'.

It is understandable that science writers want to keep things simple. But leaving out details often goes too far. Behavioural scientist and science writer James Heathers started a social media account to draw attention to a recurrent example of this problem in science reporting, namely the failure to mention that a study was done on mice and not on humans.[8] Heathers' 'justsaysinmice' project is simple. First link to a science story, such as any of these example headlines:

> Western University researchers unlock potential 'cure' for ALS.

> Vitamin D regulates microbiome-dependent cancer immunity.
>
> Groundbreaking nasal spray protects against all SARS-CoV-2 variants.
>
> Northwestern Medicine study identifies metixene as a promising breast cancer and brain metastases treatment.

Then add the phrase 'IN MICE'. Because these stories are about studies that have been carried out on mice, not humans. Heathers' point is that when news stories leave out that key information, as they often do, it is highly misleading. In this case, it creates a confusion between pre-clinical research and real clinical trials. Pre-clinical research is usually done on mice, or some other non-human species, to explore potential mechanisms that might one day lead to medical applications for humans. By contrast, a clinical trial is a real test of a developed treatment on humans, looking at efficacy and side-effects. A clinical trial is the last step before applying for approval to put a treatment on the market. Leaving out 'in mice' confuses these, which, Heathers writes, 'isn't ideal, because pre-clinical research is a billion dollars and a decade short of becoming a drug'.[9] When clarity outranks transparency, the cost is truth.

With all these cautions, caveats and uncertainties, can we trust scientists? Some sceptics reject all authority and declare, 'Do your own research'. But this is both impracticable and ill-advised. First, there is too much for one person to know. Just as there is a distribution of labour in our enormous societies, there is a distribution of knowledge and expertise. We simply cannot function as a group without some degree of trust in others to know what we don't know. That trust is crucial to achieving the heights of cooperative endeavour that humans are capable of. And by trust I do not mean accepting things on one person's say-so. I mean the trust that is warranted when communities of creative experts subject each other – and thus themselves – to rigorous error-correction. While experts are sometimes mistaken, and may never be truly certain of what they know, their errors and uncertainties pale into insignificance when we consider the incredible advances in knowledge that have changed our understanding of the world. This is not only true of the latest scientific discoveries, it also applies to the incremental building of traditional knowledge and understanding that has occurred in all societies since the beginning of humanity.

Take something seemingly simple like the cycle of the tides. Coastal and island-dwelling Indigenous societies are astute observers of the cycles and patterns of the sea. In the Torres Strait Islands, in northernmost Australia, people have depended on the sea for travel and daily livelihoods for millennia.[10] Torres Strait Islanders have become intimately familiar with the sea's behaviour and have passed on their knowledge for generations. What they know about the tides far exceeds the obvious fact that the tide comes in and goes out twice a day. They know that the time of each cycle shifts back about an hour later each day. And they know that the moon follows the same timeline. Like the tides, the moon rises about an hour later each day. They also know that just how high and low the tide goes will vary from day to day, within certain limits. They are familiar with spring tide, when high and low tide are at their extremes, and neap tide, when the difference between high and low tide is minimal. And again, they see a connection with phases of the moon. Spring tides occur when the moon is either full or new, while neap tides occur during the half-moon phase. And when the moon appears especially large in the sky – the supermoon – high tides will be especially high and low tides especially low.

This knowledge gives Torres Strait Islanders important insights that shape their daily decision-making in the most practical sense. It means, for example, that they can anticipate when neap tides occur, and thus when it is safest to dive on reefs for lobsters, and when fishing is easier and more effective:

> Elders teach that the best time to fish is during a neap (lower amplitude) tide during the First or Last Quarter Moon, rather than a spring (higher amplitude) tide during the New or Full Moon phase.
>
> The spring tides are much bigger, meaning the tidal waters rush in and out more significantly, stirring up silt and sediment on the sea floor. This clouds the water, making it harder for fish to see the bait and fishers to see the fish.
>
> The waters of spring tides also pull fish out to sea. During the smaller neap tides, the water is clearer and fish don't move as far, making them easier to see and catch.[11]

This knowledge about the tide cycles and their relation to the moon does not depend on scientific instruments but does require deep experience coupled with astute and careful observation. As we have described, knowledge of this kind is crucial for the well-being of people who depend on, and interact with, the formidable forces of the ocean.

In this way, knowledge is good when it helps us make good decisions and improve our lives. And on the principle of optimism, knowledge can always be improved. Consider two ways in which the account of the tides that we have just described could be refined.

One is greater accuracy. Observing the moon's phases can help predict whether tide extremes will be greater or less than average on a given day, but there is still variation. You could predict a neap tide but not necessarily whether today's neap tide will be more extreme than last month's. Improved knowledge could reduce this uncertainty, making your predictions more reliable and useful.

The second improvement to knowledge concerns *explanation*. Our description of the tides put forward some *correlations* between observed changes in water levels and currents, and observed phases of the moon. Such rules of thumb are often passed on in cultural wisdom, saving the younger generation the trouble of learning by trial and error. The phenomenon of 'calendar plants' is another example: on the island of Tanna in southern Vanuatu, speakers of the Nafe language monitor the native shrub they call *kapuapu* (Hedycarya dorstenioides); when its fruit appears, locals know that 'sea urchins are fat and ready to be harvested'.[12] But correlations are superficial. We can go deeper and find a model that *explains why* a correlation occurs. We may ask, then: Why is there a reliable correlation between the life cycles of *kapuapu* plants and sea urchins in Vanuatu? The answer is that both Hedycarya (the *kapuapu* plant) and Echinoidea (the urchins) follow a life cycle that is regulated by the same external cause: the earth's annual rotation around the sun. It is true that the calendar plant can provide actionable intelligence without us ever needing to know the underlying factor that helps *explain* the correlation. But explanation improves our understanding because it turns an arbitrary rule of thumb into knowledge that is broader and more powerful. A good explanation will be consistent, predictive and general.

People tend not to stop at correlations but offer explanations in the form of underlying models or narratives that say why we see the correlations we see. Let's return to the tides. What explains them? Seventeenth-century astronomer Galileo (1564–1642) was a champion of the heliocentric model – in which the earth revolves around the sun – pioneered by Nicolaus Copernicus (1473–1543). Galileo closely observed and puzzled over many aspects of the solar system, including cycles and phases of motion of the earth, moon and sun, along with other planets and stars. But he didn't believe that the moon affected the tides, despite there being a clearly visible correlation. Instead, Galileo thought that the tides were caused by the earth's motion creating a sloshing effect like water in a dinghy.

Isaac Newton – born in the year Galileo died – made a breakthrough in explaining the tides by applying his new mathematical description of *gravity*. The idea of gravitational force between heavenly bodies like planets and moons provided a natural way to explain the tides.[13] Newton posited that the moon's gravitational force on the earth created a kind of long-period wave that would 'roll around the planet as the ocean is "pulled" back and forth by the gravitational pull of the moon and the sun as these bodies interact with the Earth in their monthly and yearly orbits'.[14] This is a good explanation not only because it accounts for the specific phenomenon of the tides but because it links that explanation to a causal force – gravity – that is known to explain many other things that are independent of the tides.

Newton's theory allowed him not only to posit a causal explanation underlying the expert insights of Torres Strait Islanders, he also was able to use his planetary-system account to explain a further range of observations about the tides. For example, tidal range is different in different locations and during different seasons (inverted in the northern and southern hemispheres): 'the morning tides in winter exceed those of the evening, and the evening tides in summer exceed those of the morning; at Plymouth by the height of one foot, but at Bristol by the height of fifteen inches'.[15] Newton's theory explained these variations.

Three things are essential for understanding the cycles of the tides. First, at any moment during the earth's 24-hour rotation, the moon is facing one side of the earth. The moon's gravitational pull creates a bulge in the water on that side *and* on the opposite side of the planet, thus causing high tide on one axis and low tide on the other. Second, the moon orbits the earth once a month, on an elliptical orbit. This means that on some days the moon is closer to earth than on others. The moon's gravitational pull is greatest at the moon's *perigee* – when it is closest to earth – leading to more extreme tides on those days. Third, from earth, the position of the moon changes relative to the position of the sun, creating the effect of the moon's phases. During new moon and full moon, the sun and moon form a line with the earth (either with earth between sun and moon, or moon between sun and earth). Because the sun and moon exert gravitational pull along the same axis on those days, 'their forces will be conjoined, and bring on the greatest flood and ebb', as Newton described it (see Figure 5.2).

Figure 5.2: At full moon, the gravitational pulls of the sun and moon are aligned, their 'forces are conjoined' (Newton) causing spring tides

By contrast, when moon and sun are at right angles to the earth – that is, at half-moon – 'the sun will raise the waters which the moon depresses, and depress the waters which the moon raises, and from the difference of their forces the smallest of all tides will follow' (see Figure 5.3).[16]

Figure 5.3: At half-moon, the gravitational pulls of the sun and moon compete, 'the difference of their forces' (Newton) causing neap tides

Because these cycles run on different timelines, they can occasionally align to create even greater force upon the tides. Thus, when the earth is closest to the sun *and* the moon is closest to the earth, *and* the sun, earth and moon are in line (as in full or new moon) then the most extreme of all tides will be observed. This is not just a prediction based on correlations. It is explained by underlying causal forces of gravity and its behaviour and effects under the interaction of stars, planets and moons.

We have seen that prior to Newton, and indeed since, human groups have developed deep understandings of the tides through observation and experience. When they have offered explanations for the observed correlations, these have tended to invoke factors less like the strange and impersonal forces of gravity and more like the social forces familiar from village and family life. Here is an explanation of how the moon relates to the tides, given by Yolngu people of Arnhem Land in northern Australia:

> The Yolngu people describe Ngalindi, the Moon-man, as fat and lazy. The moon was once a young slim man (the waxing crescent Moon), who grew fat and lazy (full moon). Breaking the law, he was attacked and killed by his people (new moon). Three days later, he rose again to repeat the cycle. The Kuwema people in the Northern Territory say he grows fat at each full moon by devouring the spirits of those who disobey tribal laws.
>
> The Yolngu tell of his wives who chopped him up with their axes (waning moon). To escape, he climbs a tall tree towards the Sun, but dies from his wounds (new moon). At Yirrkala, in Arnhem Land and on Groote Eylandt, when the moon is new or full and sets at sunset or sunrise, the tides are high. When the moon is in the zenith at sunrise or sunset, the tides are low. The Aborigines believe the high tides, running into the moon as it sets into the sea, make it fat and round. When the tides are low, the water pours from the full moon into the sea and the moon becomes thin.[17]

Astrophysicist Ray Norris writes: 'If this idea seems a bit different from the modern scientific explanation involving the gravitational pull of the moon, bear in mind that, pragmatically, it works. It enables a Yolngu elder to predict the timing and height of the next tide.'[18] Norris is right that Yolngu understandings work for their local purposes, but the moon man account is more than 'a bit' different from Newton's explanation based on the theory of gravity and its causal effects. The two theories are not comparable. Newton's theory and the Yolngu theory are playing different language games.

The two stories may be equivalent for the pragmatic purpose of deciding whether to go out fishing or stay at home on a given day. The moon man story may even have the advantage of being easier to learn, remember and talk about, with its familiar human framing. And while Newton's theory is a universal one, the highly localized nature of the Yolngu story may give it special advantages outside of the domain of decision-making around activities like boating and fishing.

Such stories have been important in legal cases leading to successful sea rights claims.[19] In a case brought before the Federal Court of Australia in the early 2000s, Torres Strait Islander peoples of different islands were asked to provide evidence that the sea, not just the land, was part of their world, and that people of different islands had a shared perception and understanding of the seas as part of a larger territory common to Torres Strait Islanders. Among the evidence that helped the case succeed were myths and legends of the kind we have described here, as well as cultural practices like the Moon Dance (known as *Gedge Togia*) that was performed and explained similarly on the islands of Mabuyag and Mer, which are 200 kilometres apart.

We have taken this excursion into relations between the tides and the physics of celestial bodies to make two points.

The first is that while two theories may be equally useful for making certain predictions, they may not be equally useful as explanations. Myths that purport to explain natural phenomena can have important social functions. But they do not provide explanations in the same sense as Newton's theory of gravity does. A deeper explanation can extend to explain diverse phenomena, which before the explanation may have appeared to be unrelated. For example, using Newton's theory of gravity, one might predict that just as the moon exerts an influence on the earth's orbit, so should the planet Jupiter, albeit a smaller influence. And indeed, centuries later, this was found to be true (as discussed in what follows). A deeper explanation not only captures what was observed, it generates entirely new ideas.

The second is a deeper point about the culture of truth and knowledge. It is that advances like those by Torres Strait Islanders and by Newton in understanding the tides were improvements on what came before *and* in turn they can be improved upon. Continual improvement is possible when we sincerely commit to the idea that we have not, and will not, arrive at some final truth. We are only ever getting closer. A corollary of this commitment is that no claim to a true or correct explanation is sacred, not the Torres Strait Islanders' and not Newton's. This fits with a scientific stance of anti-authority in knowledge and of never allowing an explanation to stand as final. Even the best, most accurate and most powerful explanations are provisional. Improvement can continue when we are able to continually ask: What do we have wrong?

How can this idea be corrected? What new knowledge might this correction create in turn?

With a commitment to perpetual improvement, as William Godwin called it, stories about the moon and the sun, the planets and the stars, can get better and better. They can become more accurate and more general. For example, in the last two decades, scientists have discovered that the gravitational forces exerted by other planets in our solar system, especially the bigger planets Jupiter and Saturn, and the nearest planets such as Venus, also affect the earth, accounting for wobbles in our planet's orbit that have impacted cycles of climate change over hundreds of thousands of years. It was discovered only in the 1970s that earth's long-term swings between ice ages and glacial thaws were regulated by changes in our planet's precise orbital geometry (the shape of earth's path around the sun).[20] And only in the last decade was it confirmed that even the great planet Jupiter's gravitational pull on the earth plays a role in this.[21]

The openness to constant improvement is the basis of optimism, the idea that we can improve our understanding without limit. From this point of view, the Torres Strait Islander theory of the tides is good, Newton's gravitational theory is better, and future theories will be better again than both.[22] But these improvements are only possible if we engage in self-directed error-correction, if we keep subjecting our beliefs to critique, always considering other possibilities, including those we think are wrong. Why? Because they might, unexpectedly, turn out to be right, or even half right in some interesting way. The mindset we need is always to be striving for the truth, undeterred by knowing that we will never truly arrive.

6
THE OSTRICH INSTRUCTION

> There are ethical and moral imperatives in the search for truth and error-correction.

The philosopher William Clifford saw a pernicious tangle between ethics and incentives in the relation between truth and reasons for action.[1] He gave the example of a commercial shipowner. In Clifford's day (the mid 1800s), intercontinental travel was a dangerous undertaking done in claustrophobic craft on treacherous seas. Clifford describes a man who makes a living selling berths to passengers travelling on his ship to far shores. This shipowner isn't sure how seaworthy his ship is, and he actively chooses not to know. It's not in his economic interest to do so. When the ship goes down, drowning everyone on board, he just shrugs and collects the insurance.

Such 'stifling of doubts' – deeply unethical in Clifford's analysis – is another name for failing to strive for truth. In his defence, the shipowner may have said he had no reason to believe the ship wasn't seaworthy. But remember the lesson of confirmation bias. He also had no reason to believe it *was* seaworthy. He just chose not to test that idea. We readily believe what we want to be true, as long as we are not forced to believe otherwise. In Clifford's view, avoiding the truth is not only dangerous, it is morally wrong. In Clifford's words, 'it is wrong always, everywhere, and for anyone, to believe anything upon insufficient evidence'.

Here is another example, though in this case the damage is self-inflicted. A San Diego court in 1976 convicted Charles Jewell for trafficking 50 kilograms of marijuana hidden in a car he drove across the Mexico–US border.[2] Jewell's defence was that he didn't know about the stash. The court allowed that Jewell may not have actually seen the drugs. But consider the context. Jewell accepted a drug dealer's offer of $100 to drive the car for him. The court ruled that Jewell had engaged in wilful blindness: 'He suspected the fact [that there were drugs in the car]; he realized its probability; but he refrained from obtaining the final confirmation because he wanted in the event to be able to deny knowledge.' Jewell's ploy not only failed him, it established a legal rule known as the Ostrich Instruction, which 'informs the jury that actual knowledge and deliberate avoidance of knowledge are the same thing'.[3] (By the way, ironically, and of course, there is no truth to the idea that ostriches stick their heads in the sand.)

The moral is that seeking true reasons for action is not just the best thing to do, it is the right thing to do. Deliberately avoiding knowledge may at times seem strategic, but according to Clifford it is the enemy of the good.

Strategically omitting the truth is a well-known strategy for deception. It is not the same as lying, but it is the next best thing. Consider the case of Samuel Bronston,[4] New York-based movie producer who made films in the 1950s and 1960s in various European locations.

Bronston's company filed for federal bankruptcy protection in the United States in 1964. He was questioned under oath during the hearing. Here was the key exchange:

Q: Do you have any bank accounts in Swiss banks, Mr. Bronston?
A: No, sir.
Q: Have you ever?
A: The company had an account there for about six months, in Zurich.

Bronston answered the first question directly and truthfully. He did not have a Swiss bank account at the time. He did, however, previously have an account in Geneva, between October 1959 and June 1964. So, Bronston's answer to the second question was evasive at best. He could have answered with a direct and truthful 'Yes'. This, of course, would have incriminated him. So instead, he answered about a company account, not a personal account. What he said was the truth, but not the whole truth.

When it was discovered that Bronston *had* previously held a Swiss bank account, he was charged and found guilty of perjury by the US District Court for the Southern District of New York. Bronston appealed but the Second Circuit affirmed the conviction, arguing that 'witnesses should not be able to intentionally mislead questioners with half-truths' and that Bronston's answer contained a 'lie by negative implication'.[5] But in the end, the Supreme Court reversed the decision and overturned the perjury conviction 'because his answer, while misleading and unresponsive, was literally true'.

This established what is now known as the literal truth defence. The Supreme Court reasoned that courtroom testimony is a unique language game. Juries are not entitled to infer negative implications from an evasive answer in the same way they might in casual conversation. The Court ruled that it is the questioner's responsibility to recognize when a witness is being evasive and to 'bring the witness back to the mark'.[6] But this is too much to ask when faced with a skilled player of the game. Under the current conditions established by the Bronston case, 'a sophisticated defendant can dodge a perjury charge by providing a literally true answer while omitting pertinent information'.[7]

The Bronston case shows that leaving important information out can effectively transform a true statement into a lie. But context matters. Sometimes it is good not to know certain information. Withholding information, whether from oneself or someone else, can be a form of *strategic unknowing*.[8] There are many things we would prefer remain unknown. The reasons for this are not all bad. For example, strategic unknowing underpins many practices that aim to avoid discrimination, corruption or conflicts of interest.

In auditions for orchestras, musicians have long been required to remain behind a screen to avoid bias, for example based on gender or age.[9] When scientific research submissions are sent for peer review before publication, they are often anonymized, to avoid discrimination based on such things as seniority, personal animosity, competition and conflicts of interest. A corollary of this bias-reducing function of strategic unknowing is that it can be used in defending oneself against accusations of wrongdoing. If the gender of candidates was withheld from me as chair of a selection committee, I can truthfully say that gender was not a factor in my decision.

A downside of this mechanism of deniability from unknowing is that it may be abused. If CEOs intentionally shield themselves from their company's illegal dealings, they can deny involvement (and let some underling take the fall). This doesn't always work. In 2012, British pharmaceutical giant GlaxoSmithKline was ordered by American authorities to pay a fine of three billion US dollars for committing fraud, specifically by neglecting to report safety information that might have harmed the sales of some of their most profitable pharmaceuticals.[10] By not reporting data that would have drawn attention to drug safety issues, they maximized financial profits. But covering up that information was illegal and had potential public health risks. The company paid handsomely.

Another kind of case turns on information which some may prefer not to know. In March 1999,[11] John Kelly, Managing Director of Lenah Game Meats in the Australian state of Tasmania, was embroiled in a court fight over his company's methods of slaughtering wild game. The Australian Broadcasting Commission (ABC) had obtained a secretly recorded video of the possum-killing operations at Kelly's premises and were notifying him that scenes were to be aired on the ABC's national news programme, *The 7.30 Report*. The ABC got the video from Animal Liberation Limited, who in turn got it from someone who had trespassed in order to install hidden cameras inside Kelly's premises. In his bid to block the recording being broadcast, Kelly started a legal case that would ultimately reach the High Court of Australia.

High Court records noted: 'The methods by which the possums are killed, although lawful, are objected to by some people, including people associated with Animal Liberation Limited, on the ground that they are cruel.'[12] The point of making the recording was to bring these methods to public attention, based on the assumption that the scenes would upset people, and would in turn influence their opinions about the meat industry. Kelly, assuming the same thing, reasoned that this was precisely why the recording should not be aired:

> The distribution and publication of this film is likely to adversely and substantially affect the [respondent's] business. The film is of the most gruesome parts of the [respondent's] brush tail possum processing operation. It shows possums being stunned and then having their throats cut. It is likely to arouse public disquiet, perhaps even anger, at the way in which the [respondent] conducts its lawful business. This is no different from any animal slaughtering operation in Australia, which is normally hidden from public view.

This reasoning assumes that members of the public would change their behaviour if they learned of the truth. Both sides agree on this point. The difference in their views is whether they believe it would be a good thing or a bad thing were people to see something that is at once upsetting and normally hidden from public view.

In the Lenah Game Meats case, unlike with GlaxoSmithKline's duty of disclosure, the firm was not obliged to provide video recordings of their operations to the public or to otherwise reveal the details of their practices, as long as their operations were conducted lawfully.

Withholding relevant information is one of the many ways in which public discourse has a complicated relationship with the truth. How can we determine what information is need-to-know? Do meat eaters need to know what the lawful business of meat production looks like? Kelly's lawyers argued to the High Court that publishing the scenes would be an invasion of the firm's privacy. But the ABC won the case. While the acts took place on private land, they were not 'relevantly private' as far as the law was concerned. The judgment was that an act cannot be held private 'simply because the owner of land would prefer that it were unobserved'.

Alongside the question of whether meat eaters need to see what is normally hidden, there is the question of whether they *want* to see it. Most would presumably rather not, and so Lenah Game Meats' argument against airing the recording might in a sense have also had their consumers' preferences in mind. But remember the Ostrich Instruction:

> You may infer knowledge from a combination of suspicion and indifference to the truth. If you find that a person had a strong suspicion that things were not what they seemed or that someone had withheld some important facts yet shut his eyes for fear that he would learn, you may conclude that he acted knowingly.[13]

If a known drug dealer pays you to bring a package into the country, you can't just refrain from looking inside it so that later you can say truthfully that you didn't know the drugs were there. You might not have seen them with your own eyes, but a court of law will treat you as having known they were there anyway. This points to another target of hidden-camera activism: not the industry but the consumers, whose deliberate avoidance of knowledge would be sabotaged by seeing the recordings.

No party promotes illegal activities per se, but some would argue that there is a trade-off. Some are willing to break one law to stop other people from breaking another. This trade-off was central to discussions in the 2018 New South Wales (Australia) Government Select Committee on Landowner Protection from Unauthorised Filming or Surveillance. The committee was established 'to inquire into and report on the extent of protection for landowners from unauthorised filming or surveillance'.[14] The Committee received numerous submissions. Compare these two excerpts:

Animal Liberation Limited submission: Attempts to gag the collection of materials obtained by private animal cruelty investigators significantly diminishes the capacity of the consumer to be reliably aware of practices inherent in the production of animal products. Given attempts occasionally made by animal enterprises to provide consumers with misleading or deceptive information, such investigations are often the only form of transparent information concerning animal enterprises that the public have access to.

Australian Pork Limited submission: Pig producers undertaking lawful businesses are being targeted by activist vigilantes intent on undertaking illegal activities (e.g. trespass) with the sole objective of causing the industry harm, and stop consumers eating pork ... a person who suspects they have witnessed a crime, namely animal cruelty, should immediately present their evidence to authorities so that any alleged crime can be

> investigated and any perpetrators brought to justice in a timely fashion. ... Protections could be made available for individuals who act in good faith in an attempt to expose criminal activity, as distinct from individuals who are aware that no criminal activity is being committed, yet wish to trespass on and disrupt law abiding businesses.

The difference in perspective could not be starker. In theory, we might expect a formal inquiry to create a marketplace of ideas, of the kind that philosopher John Stuart Mill argued would create conditions in which the best decisions would prevail.[15] But instead of a market for ideas we have a market for justifications.[16] People frame their understandings of reality in line with their own incentives.

The problem with incentives is that they feed well-known cognitive biases such as the confirmation bias, where people look for evidence to confirm what they already think is true. This is in direct conflict with a core principle of the scientific method of approaching truth: seeking to *dis*confirm one's hypotheses in order to be able to say that those hypotheses have been successfully tested. A form of discourse in which arguments are built directly in the service of in-place policies is not likely to take us closer to truth.

In the quest for knowledge to guide us towards better decision-making, the problem of ignorance or unknowing is as serious as the problem of false belief. When it comes to uncomfortable truths, it is not clear that their being normally hidden from public view is grounds for keeping them hidden. For example, a key factor in ending the Vietnam War was the widespread change in public opinion that occurred after confronting images of the far-away conflict hit the evening news. Sometimes the problem is not that citizens are being kept in the dark about things they would want to know. Sometimes we prefer not to know things that implicate us, whether it be the human cost of a distant political campaign or the reality of how meat is produced behind closed doors. Should we intentionally look away from things that we have a stake in, say through our practices as voters or as consumers? Or do we have a responsibility to confront ourselves with certain truths that we know, if only deep down, we are implicated in?

The benefits of avoiding knowledge in ways we have reviewed so far have been associated with accountability. People seek not to know precisely in order that they can later attest truthfully that they didn't know. But there are other practical benefits from avoiding certain knowledge. Often, stripping away extraneous information makes it easier to process and remember information.

Consider the breakthrough that was Harry Beck's original 1933 London tube map.[17] Beck was an English draughtsman born in 1902. The maps of the underground lines in the early 20th century showed the true geographical layout of the lines (see Figure 6.1).

Beck felt that much of this information was extraneous and distracting, and that map users wanted action-relevant practical information. They wanted to see the stations in order. And they wanted to see where

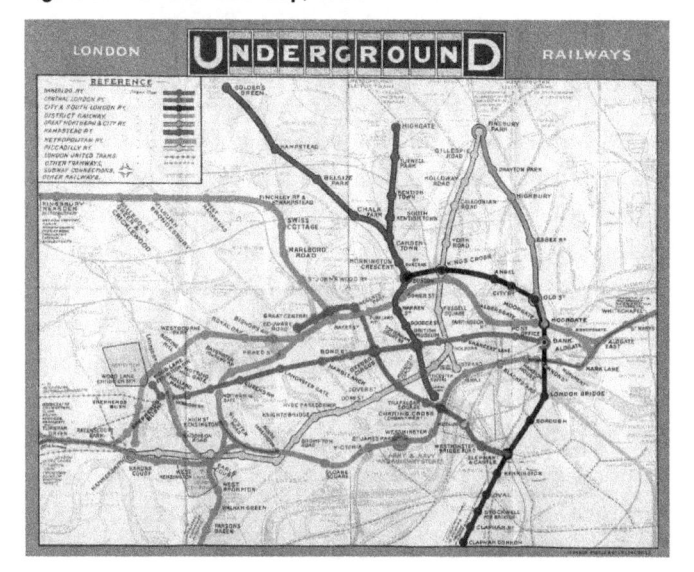

Figure 6.1: London tube map, 1908

they could change trains. The 'true' maps had too much information. Inspired by a schematic drawing of an electrical circuit, Beck created the first version of the tube map, with its straight lines, evenly spaced stations and consistent angles.

The fact that these lines, spacings and angles were not 'true' to the physical layout of the network did not mean they were not useful. The opposite was true. Removing information improved the maps. Beck showed that certain facts are irrelevant – indeed distracting – and so can be left out. But this does not mean that Beck's map contained falsehoods. Rather, the new map was a direct answer to commuters' questions. It was designed for a specific information market.

While the tube map principle is purely one of goal-oriented efficiency, other cases we have discussed illustrate the ethically charged nature of selective knowledge. A meat eater may not want to know how their food is killed, but someone might argue that they *should* know. An orchestra director may want to know if the violinist behind the audition screen is a man or a woman, or may want to know their skin colour, but someone might argue that they *should not* know. Rules about selective knowledge are, in part, about our values.

Is it bad to selectively withhold the truth? 'Information wants to be free', say many activists seeking openness and transparency.[18] 'Information is the currency of democracy',[19] say those who want to have free access to all information about the government's dealings. 'True information does good' was the response from publisher Julian Assange, when asked, 'Is there anything you wouldn't leak?'[20]

Yet even Assange acknowledges that harms can come from releasing information. This is why there are constraints on what is available under the Freedom of Information Act. Most people acknowledge that secrecy is sometimes necessary, as expressed here by journalism scholar Michael Schudson:[21]

> There really are military secrets that should not fall into the hands of fanatics, practical jokers, or deranged people. There really is a need for government decision-makers to be able to trust in the confidentiality of their meetings and of their electronic communications if there is to be a free flow of conversation among them.

But behind any consensus about the occasional need for secrecy, people vehemently disagree about when and where that need arises. Many baulk at freedom of information when it impinges on their privacy. Journalist Glenn Greenwald describes the problem:[22]

> As I've debated this issue around the world, every single time somebody has said to me, 'I don't really worry about invasions of privacy because I don't have anything to hide', I always say the same thing to them. I get out a pen, I write down my email address. I say, 'Here's my email address. What I want you to do when you get home is email me the passwords to all of your email accounts, not just the nice, respectable work one in your name, but all of them, because I want to be able to just troll through what it is you're doing online, read what I want to read and publish whatever I find interesting. After all, if you're not a bad person, if you're doing nothing wrong, you should have nothing to hide.' Not a single person has taken me up on that offer.

If you are like those people and you agree that *some* truths are better kept secret, then no matter where you stand on the degree to which 'information should be free', you are still faced with the puzzle of where to draw the line.

We argued earlier in this book that if something is true, that can make it a *good reason* for action. But of course this doesn't mean that the *actions* in question will be good, morally or otherwise. Through action, truth has consequences. Truths themselves are neutral but our decisions to act upon those truths confront us with moral and ethical questions. Here we confront the unsolved dilemma of the scout. You have discovered the truth. Now what?

7
MINDFUL OPTIMISM

How can we realize the ideal of what truth is for?
Answer: Foster the culture of intellectual humility and mindful optimism.

We need to know what is true, so that we may use that knowledge to make good decisions. We need this in the information age, just as we have needed it since the dawn of our species. How do we ensure that we know the truth? As individuals, we must each develop the skill, and the disposition, to find errors in our own knowledge or beliefs, and to correct them. As communities, we must collectively commit to an error-correcting future. I argue that this requires *mindful optimism*: the conscious and deliberate commitment to error-correction, in oneself as much as in others, as a means for perpetual improvement of knowledge and action.

This means working against the enemies of truth. There is bias: I'm wrong but I don't know it. There is laziness: So far I haven't needed to know if I'm wrong. There is wishful thinking: This is true because I want it to be. There is arrogance: There is no way I'm wrong. There is identitarianism: I'm right because of who I am. And there is authoritarianism: I'm right because I say so.

These enemies of truth can be kept at bay – though not without eternal vigilance – by shared commitment to a mode of thinking and interacting that is sometimes called rationalism. In philosopher Karl Popper's words: 'Rationalism is an attitude of readiness to listen to critical arguments and to learn from experience. It is fundamentally an attitude of admitting that "*I may be wrong and you may be right, and by an effort, we may get nearer to the truth*".'[1] Do not misunderstand what Popper is saying. It is not that I should defer to you. Because just as I may be wrong, so too may you. Just as I have no authority to dictate what is true, neither do you. The key is that we can *together* embrace and relish the possibility that *we* are wrong, and then actively seek out reasons to change our own minds, helping each other to improve. We may need to use our most creative powers to find those reasons. And we should be willing to self-correct and be able to recognize when circumstances demand that we do so. This radically decentralized and anti-authoritarian approach to knowledge is what created the advances in knowledge and practice that have continued to improve people's lives in ways especially noticeable over recent centuries.[2]

Author and commentator Jonathan Rauch describes two 'social rules' that echo Popper's idea of what it means to seek the truth.[3] In our species' recent history, these rules 'supplanted intellectual authoritarianism' and together they define foundations of the brand of optimism known variously as Enlightenment thinking, rationality or liberal science.

First is *the sceptical rule*: 'No one gets the final say.' This means that 'no idea can ever have any claim to be exempt from criticism by anyone'. This does not mean that all claims to truth are wrong. It means that all claims to truth *might* be wrong, even ones that we are very confident about, or that are made by very wise people. Therefore, we should always allow critique of those claims to be heard.

Second is *the empirical rule*: 'No one has special authority.' This means that 'no one gets special say simply on the basis of who he happens to be'.[4] The rule is empirical because it emphasizes the need to provide evidence when making a claim. It sets aside the status of the person who makes that claim.

These rules do not tell you how to think. They are norms for coordination and cooperation. If we could together embrace the combination of intellectual rigour and humility, grounded in a shared readiness to listen, then we could realize the ideal of a 'community of error-seeking inquirers accountable to each other but never to any particular authority'.[5]

A term for the idea I have just referenced is intellectual humility. It is intellectual because it means thinking carefully and rigorously, with the goal of reaching new knowledge and understanding. It is humility because it means assuming that we could be wrong.

It means being willing to listen and being willing to be corrected.

As Popper argued, winning in a debate is of no help to the truth-seeker. Through intellectual humility and mindful optimism, the goal is to improve knowledge – not just for ourselves but for everyone – by taking seriously the ideas of those whose views we think are wrong. But simply possessing intellectual humility is not enough. Intellectual humility needs to be exercised, like a muscle. It is antifragile.[6] This means it gets stronger the more it is used, and without use it becomes weaker and more prone to failure. How do we exercise our intellectual humility? The answer is by subjecting our views to rigorous criticism.

You may be open-minded, but if you are not exposed to diverse evidence and viewpoints that challenge your assumptions and inject new ideas, you will find it hard to innovate and improve. As the philosopher John Stuart Mill wrote, 'he who knows only his side of the case knows little of that'. Mill warned that however true an opinion may be, 'if it is not fully, frequently, and fearlessly discussed, it will be held as a dead dogma, not a living truth'.[7] This rule for a healthy information ecology also holds for ecosystems in biology, where monoculture leads to sterility or collapse, and where too much of something can turn even a healthy substance into a toxic pollutant. It is also true of the process of evolution, where diversity in populations ensures that limits are being tried, tested and surpassed. And it is true of the evolution of ideas. Diversity creates competition, and competition leads to improvement.

Let me emphasize that 'diversity' here means diversity of data and ideas, not diversity of the people who communicate them per se. The advantage of having a diversity of input is independent from the politics of representing under-represented social groups (though such representation may make diversity of input more likely). Remember the empirical rule. To find truth, focus on the content of potential knowledge, not on the properties of the people who convey it.

One way to understand the need for a diverse information ecology in the search for truth is to focus on the kinds of minds we bring to this process. Our thinking is uniquely flexible but it can become staid and brittle if it gets the same old input every day. To avoid this, we need to actively seek noise injections for the mind.[8] The human mind is an elite learning-based decision machine, but our performance is only as good as the data we learn from. If our experience is not diverse, our minds suffer from what data scientists call *overfitting*. This is what happens when a model 'pays too much attention to the particular data set it is trained on, causing it to perform poorly on unseen data'.[9]

Suppose you are training a machine-learning algorithm to recognize dogs in images online. You start by giving it a training set of images, labelled with 'dog' whenever a dog appears. The computer infers a model from this input. But suppose that every dog in your training set happens to be a husky. Your model becomes flawless at picking out huskies but fails when it later sees a Dobermann or a beagle. The Internet contains billions of images of hundreds of dog breeds, many of which look very different from huskies.

Engineers try to combat overfitting in two ways. One is to ensure that the training data – that is, whatever you experience during a period of learning – shows as much variety as possible. The model improves when it learns from a more representative sample of the full space of possibilities. The lesson is to think ahead and see to it that huskies aren't the only breed representing 'dogs' in your training data. Make sure your model learns on the broadest range of examples possible.

A second way to combat overfitting is to introduce random noise into the system as it learns. It is good to be surprised by weirdness, not because there is necessarily any value in the strange or unexpected thing itself (though there may be), but because surprises keep you alert and challenged, and can direct you to possibilities you would not have imagined. Consider the approach that jazz musicians use when they face the overfitting problem (see Figure 7.1).

Jazz performance requires players to constantly come up with original, unanticipated ideas and execute them in real time. But as anthropologist Eitan Wilf writes, habit and predictability can stifle creativity.[10] To solve this, musicians can draw on random events for inspiration. In one of Wilf's examples, jazz students in class hear a car horn from the street outside, and then try to match the sound with their instruments.[11] With this technique, a random noise is seized upon as an escape hatch for creative action.

Figure 7.1: Jazz musician Sidney Bechet, New York, c. November 1946

A similar example comes from psychotherapy. The process sometimes gets bogged down, with both patient and therapist running out of ideas. Therapist Susan Rako describes a solution that taps into the random outcomes of consulting the I Ching, an ancient Chinese 'oracle' practice that uses a kind of coin-toss system to find answers to problems.[12] Rako reports that her patients can be 'creatively stimulated' by the hatch-opening experience of reading the I Ching, in a process not unlike the random car-horn sound that relieves the jazz player's creative block.

The more comfortable and confident we become, the less we pay attention. The more predictable the situation, the less we analyse it. The more obvious a next step appears, the less we consider our options. It is true that all of this can save us effort. But any benefits are outweighed by a distinct disadvantage: the comfort of familiarity is an off-switch for the mind.

How, then, can we maintain an information ecology that keeps surprising and challenging us? I want to emphasize two parts of a solution. The first is to actively expand our horizons by learning about ways of thinking other than our own. The second is to encourage and embrace candid criticism and the 'clash of cultures' that results.[13]

Languages, cultures and value systems unlike our own are rich sources of the precious diversity and noise that help prevent cognitive overfitting. Each language, and each culture, is rich and complex and must be learned, piece by piece, over many years. The early years of our lives are devoted almost wholly to this learning. Once we have acquired a human language, and a shared set of values and ideals, these are our master keys to the societies in which we live. But once we have cleared the hurdle of admission to our home group, our learning slows down, mainly because we are too occupied with life to keep learning. Our default settings for thinking, communicating, reasoning and decision-making become entrenched, and increasingly less likely to be revised or refined.[14]

We can counteract this slowing-down of learning by accessing the greatest-known source of noise injections for the mind: namely, other languages and cultures. Mid-20th-century linguistic anthropologist Benjamin Lee Whorf said that when you only know one language, or one type of language, you are like someone with 'the physiological defect of being able to see only the colour blue'.[15] Such a person would 'hardly be able to formulate the rule that they saw only blue'. Whorf wrote, 'In order to formulate the rule or norm of seeing only blue, they would need exceptional moments in which they saw other colours.' Whorf argued that there was a way to seek out these exceptional moments. It is to learn languages unlike our own.

So, here is how to avoid the perils of overfitting. Learn other languages. Read other books. Go to other places. Mix in other circles. Every unfamiliar experience gives you another escape hatch, a potential path to error-correction. Just as our dreams give us respite from the rigid normalcy of daily routine,[16] so in our waking hours must we find the jolts that our antifragile minds so badly need.

Another step towards increasing our diversity of input is to promote the value of frank, unvarnished speech. This idea is captured in the Ancient Greek term *parrhesia*: 'frankly saying to others what they may not want to hear'.[17] This is complemented by *isegoria*, the right of equal speech, the right of each person to be heard.[18]

Whether people get to talk, and what they get to say when they do talk, can vary with the fashions of the day. In recent times, as research in the United States finds, there has been 'a growing culture of intolerance towards objectionable speech'.[19] But on balance, tolerating objectionable speech is good. This is because freedom of *thought alone* is not enough.

For free ideas to help with collective error-correction, they must be *made public*. Key Enlightenment thinkers emphasized this point:[20] Immanuel Kant's 1784 essay 'What is Enlightenment?' called for the 'freedom to make a *public use* of one's reason' (emphasis in original); John Stuart Mill's 1859 essay 'On Liberty' viewed 'the liberty of *expressing and publishing* opinions' as 'practically inseparable' from free thought (emphasis added).

How do we create an environment in which free and frank speech are fostered? Two things are needed. One is that people should have the courage to say what is on their mind. The other is that listeners should show that they value, not just tolerate, free and sometimes objectionable speech.

Remember that the 'final argument' is force. The alternatives to speech are violence and fear. To pick one illustrative example out of too many to count, consider the story of Dutch film director Theo van Gogh (1957–2004). Van Gogh was harshly critical of Islam. Soon after the release of his 2004 film *Submission*, a strident statement against the treatment of women in Islamic countries, he was assassinated for his views. Twenty-six-year-old Mohammed Bouyeri ambushed van Gogh on an Amsterdam street and shot him multiple times, before attempting to decapitate him, and finally pinning a note to his chest with a fillet knife as he lay dying.[21]

People may have disagreed with van Gogh's ideas and values. He was both hated and loved in Dutch society for the things he said. But words are in the realm of social reality. They may offend. They may even cause pain. But they are not violence. Unlike bullets, knives and cannons, words can deliver no final argument.

Yet words are confused more and more with violence in political and academic discourse today.[22] What was once a claim based on a feeling of offence ('don't say that, it offends me') has now become medicalized as harm ('don't say that, it damages my mental health').[23] The solution is to distinguish between the things about ourselves that we can control versus those we can't. This is the distinction between the social reality of words and the physical reality of violence.

Popper suggested that while the clash of cultures can be bracing, 'we may learn to enjoy it'.[24] And that is the thing about words. We *learn* them. We *learn* their meanings, and we *learn* how to respond to them. Otherwise, words are just sounds, or marks on a page. They cannot harm us. Just as we can learn what words mean, we can learn to be less offended by them. We can learn to resist the urge to kill people for them. We can learn to listen and think. We can learn never to confuse social reality and brute reality.

When we encounter untempered speech, we don't have to like it. We don't have to celebrate it. But there are reasons to allow it, and indeed encourage it. One reason is that it might help us correct our errors. Another is that it will keep us informed about what people in our world are thinking. And third, if we feel confident that an objectionable *parrhesiastes* or say-it-all[25] will leave the scene without a knife in his chest then this is a welcome sign that we are living in an anti-authoritarian culture that values error-correction, creativity and progress.

Let me emphasize that free speech – a necessary condition for the combination of creativity and criticism that leads us in the direction of truth – is insufficient on its own. All speech can easily be coopted for purely signalling purposes. As philosopher Teresa Bejan puts it (emphasis in original): '[W]hat passes for "free speech" today strikes me as singularly unconcerned with persuading anyone. We speak our minds *not* to change the minds of our opponents, but to tell our friends – and enemies – which side we're on.'[26] Let you and me both have the right to think and speak with creativity and wildness, and the right to subject the other's wild thoughts to unbuttoned critique. And let that critique be as constructive and charitable as it is rigorous and severe. As the author Salman Rushdie has insisted, without freedom of expression in public, there can be no freedom of thought in the privacy of your mind. 'The moment you declare a set of ideas to be immune from criticism, satire, derision, or contempt, freedom of thought becomes impossible.'[27] Here is Rushdie's rule of thumb: 'You never personalize, but you have absolutely no respect for people's opinions.' And by 'no respect' he means the very highest respect: taking what is said purely on its merits, by separating its content entirely from the person who says it.

***

Humans are capable of the remarkable feat of collective error-correction. We do it by focusing our attention on our own beliefs and thoughts, evaluating them, and deliberately overriding them when needed. And with language we socialize the process, making it vastly more efficient and effective. This is the culture of mindful optimism.

Possibly the single greatest threat to this ideal is the tendency to put tribe before truth. But ingeniously, mindful optimism has an inbuilt mechanism for solving this problem. The solution is to *define our tribe by the search for truth*. Let us be the people who want to know the truth more than we want to be right.

NOTES

Preface

1. Laos will be mentioned more than once among the examples given in this book. It is a place I know intimately, having spent many years conducting research there and in surrounding areas on the languages and cultures of mainland Southeast Asia.
2. The term 'alignment problem' echoes the title of Brian Christian's 2020 book on the problem of aligning AI systems and human values. Brian Christian, *The Alignment Problem: Machine Learning and Human Values* (W.W. Norton & Company, 2020).
3. David Deutsch, *The Beginning of Infinity: Explanations that Transform the World* (Penguin, 2011), p. 56.
4. Deutsch, *The Beginning of Infinity*, p. 212. I note that the word 'evils' here can be misleading. For me, it refers here simply to things we would have avoided if we had more knowledge. It does not mean that morally evil people are necessarily ignorant, nor vice versa.
5. For example, according to philosopher Colin McGinn, human consciousness is a *mystery*, meaning that our inherent mental limitations prevent us from being ever able to understand it. See Colin McGinn, 'Can We Solve the Mind–Body Problem?', *Mind* 98(391) (1989), pp. 349–366. McGinn writes that it is 'deplorably anthropocentric to insist that reality be constrained by what the human mind can conceive' (p. 366). See also Nicholas G. Carr, 'Mysterianism', *Edge*, 2017, https://www.edge.org/response-detail/27017. McGinn usefully distinguishes between four sorts of question: problems (questions we can solve, in principle), mysteries (questions we cannot solve, not even in principle), illusions (pseudo-questions) and issues (ethical and similar questions that have no objective answer) (Colin McGinn, *Problems in Philosophy: The Limits of Inquiry* [Blackwell, 1993], p. 3).

NOTES

Chapter 1

1. John R. Searle, *The Construction of Social Reality* (The Free Press, 1995).
2. Alfred Tarski, 'The Semantic Conception of Truth and the Foundations of Semantics', *Philosophy and Phenomenological Research* 4 (1944), pp. 341–376.
3. This section draws on Scott A. Snook, *Friendly Fire: The Accidental Shootdown of U.S. Black Hawks over Northern Iraq* (Princeton University Press, 2000).
4. Snook, *Friendly Fire*, p. 163: 'The Airspace Control Order (ACO) seems clear: "No aircraft will enter the TAOR ['Tactical Area of Responsibility'] until the fighters with AI [air interrogation] radars have sanitized the TAOR." However, to Army aviators in Eagle Flight, the word "aircraft" did not include helicopters. ... Army aviators had good reason to believe that this "fighter sweep" restriction did not apply to them.' See also the discussion in Jacques Crémer, Luis Garicano and Andrea Prat, 'Language and the Theory of the Firm', *The Quarterly Journal of Economics* 122(1) (2007), pp. 373–407, at p. 374.
5. The specific wording of the quote as cited here is from the feature film *Becket* (Paramount Pictures, 1964), starring Richard Burton and Peter O'Toole. See Jonathan McGovern, 'The Origin of the Phrase "Will no one rid me of this turbulent priest?"', *Notes and Queries* 68(3) (2021), p. 266.
6. *Wolf of Wall Street* (Paramount Pictures, 2013). A clip of the scene can be found here: https://www.youtube.com/watch?v=vYyzfa4aKDM from 3:50.
7. For experimental studies of the psychological strategies and game theory that underlie indirect speech, see Steven Pinker, Martin A. Nowak and James J. Lee. 'The Logic of Indirect Speech', *Proceedings of the National Academy of Sciences* 105(3) (2008), pp. 833–838 and James J. Lee and Steven Pinker, 'Rationales for Indirect Speech: The Theory of the Strategic Speaker', *Psychological Review* 117(3) (2010), pp. 785–807.
8. Patti Murphy and David Stout, 'Idaho Senator Says He Regrets Guilty Plea in Restroom Incident', *New York Times*, 29 August 2007, https://www.nytimes.com/2007/08/29/washington/29craig.html. For further information and links see https://en.wikipedia.org/wiki/Larry_Craig_scandal.
9. Giovanni Rossi, Mark Dingemanse, Simeon Floyd, Julija Baranova, Joe Blythe, ... and N.J. Enfield, 'Shared Cross-Cultural Principles

10. Paul Drew, 'Contested Evidence in Courtroom Cross-examination: The Case of a Trial for Rape', in Paul Drew and John Heritage (eds) *Talk at Work: Interaction in Institutional Settings* (Cambridge University Press, 1992), pp. 470–520. Quote is from p. 477.
11. Drew, 'Contested Evidence in Courtroom Cross-examination', p. 489.
12. Drew, 'Contested Evidence in Courtroom Cross-examination', p. 487.
13. This point is explored in detail in N.J. Enfield, *Language vs. Reality: Why Language Is Good for Lawyers and Bad for Scientists* (MIT Press, 2022).
14. The following draws on a discussion in the opening paragraphs of N.J. Enfield, *The Utility of Meaning* (Oxford University Press, 2015).
15. Émile Durkheim, *The Elementary Forms of Religious Life* (The Free Press, 1995, translation of original in French, 1912), p. 133.

Chapter 2

1. To clarify, saying that truth is a good basis for action does not entail that it is necessarily a basis for good action. (What people choose to do with their knowledge is an ethical conundrum, beyond our scope here.) The question of what is good is the subject of libraries of philosophical literature on morality and ethics. Here, and mostly in this book, I use the word 'good' not in the moral sense of the opposite of evil, but in the more functional sense that philosopher Philippa Foot suggests we would apply when considering how 'good' the roots of a particular oak tree are. We would say 'it has good roots because they are as sturdy and deep as an oak's roots should be', as opposed to roots that are 'spindly and all near the surface'; Philippa Foot, *Natural Goodness* (Clarendon Press, 2001), p. 46.
2. Julia Galef, *The Scout Mindset: Why Some People See Things Clearly and Others Don't* (Portfolio, 2021). The psychologist Jonathan Haidt has made a similar distinction, which he calls discover mode and defend mode: Jonathan Haidt, *The Anxious Generation: How the Great Rewiring of Childhood Is Causing an Epidemic of Mental Illness* (Allen Lane, 2024).
3. Martin Stevens, 'Nature's Cheats: How Animals and Plants Trick and Deceive', *The Conversation*, 15 March 2016,

NOTES

        https://theconversation.com/natures-cheats-how-animals-and-plants-trick-and-deceive-55323.

4   Gossip is a basic function of language the world over. See Gary Alan Fine and Ralph L. Rosnow, 'Gossip, Gossipers, Gossiping', *Personality and Social Psychology Bulletin* 4(1) (1978), pp. 161–168. Robin I.M. Dunbar, 'Gossip in Evolutionary Perspective', *Review of General Psychology* 8(2) (2004), pp. 100–110.

5   Tania A. Reynolds, Jon K. Maner and Roy F. Baumeister, 'Bless Her Heart: Gossip Phrased with Concern Provides Advantages in Female Intrasexual Competition', *Journal of Experimental Social Psychology* 116 (2025), pp. 1–12.

6   This can't be taken as a blanket statement, for two reasons. (1) Children believe in Santa Claus but would we say that is *immoral*? (2) Clifford specifies that evidence must 'be sufficient', but how much evidence is enough? In science, our knowledge is never complete, yet we can act on partial knowledge with good effect.

7   William K. Clifford, 'The Ethics of Belief', *Contemporary Review*, 29 (January 1877), pp. 289–309.

8   Ilya Somin, *Democracy and Political Ignorance: Why Smaller Government Is Smarter* (Stanford Law Books, 2013), p. 6.

9   Sis Iboy's story is discussed on p. 739 of Nora England, 'Mayan Language Revival and Revitalization Politics', *American Anthropologist* 105(4) (2003), pp. 733–743.

10   The distinction between dialects and languages is often obvious: Japanese and Spanish are two separate languages, while British and American English are dialects of one language, English. But there is a grey area, which is complicated by politics: Mandarin speakers cannot easily understand Cantonese yet the languages are considered to be 'dialects' of Chinese (for Chinese unity), while Dutch and Flemish are almost the same yet they are often regarded as separate 'languages' because they are spoken in separate nation-states (the Netherlands and Belgium).

11   Peter Boghossian, *Fear of Knowledge: Against Relativism and Constructivism* (Oxford University Press, 2006).

12   Boghossian, *Fear of Knowledge*, p. 1.

13   One way to think about these stories is that they should be taken seriously but not literally. Fictional stories can convey fundamental ideas or lessons while obviously not claiming to be true. What I am warning against here is the error of taking the literal meaning of a story as a reason for action.

14 Carlo Ginzburg, *Clues, Myths, and the Historical Method* (Johns Hopkins University Press, 1989). For a rich and extensive discussion of witches and witchcraft, in Europe especially, see Ronald Hutton, *The Witch: A History of Fear, from Ancient Times to the Present* (Yale University Press, 2017).
15 https://www.iaewh.com/.
16 https://www.whrin.org/.

Chapter 3

1 John R. Searle, *Making the Social World: The Structure of Human Civilization* (Oxford University Press, 2010).
2 E.E. Evans-Pritchard, 'Customs and Beliefs Relating to Twins Among the Nilotic Nuer', *The Uganda Journal* (1936), pp. 230–238. Quote from p. 236. See also E.E. Evans-Pritchard, *Nuer Religion* (Oxford University Press, 1956), pp. 128ff.
3 Max Weber, *Wirtschaft und Gesellschaft* (J.C.B. Mohr, 1921). English translation: Max Weber, *Economy and Society* (University of California Press, 1978).
4 Chris Knight, Camilla Power and Ian Watts, 'The Human Symbolic Revolution: A Darwinian Account', *Cambridge Archaeological Journal* 5(1) (1995), pp. 75–114.
5 Dan Sperber, *Rethinking Symbolism* (Cambridge University Press, 1975).
6 Ludwig Wittgenstein, *Philosophical Investigations* (Basil Blackwell, 1953).
7 It is possible that the belief is self-fulfilling: that is, having the tattoo makes people less likely to want to harm you (that is, because your tattoo discourages or frightens them). But to claim that the tattoo literally 'stops bullets' is to invoke magic, defined by anthropologist Claude Lévi-Strauss as 'the naturalization of human actions' or the 'physiomorphism of man', the idea that 'man can intervene in natural determinism to complete or modify its course'. Claude Lévi-Strauss, *The Savage Mind* (Weidenfeld & Nicolson, 1966), p. 221.
8 See Tom Nichols, *The Death of Expertise*, 2nd edition (Cambridge University Press, 2024).
9 From a tweet: @DavidDeutschOxf, 11 May 2018: https://x.com/DavidDeutschOxf/status/994918776381505538.
10 'Oversight Hearing on Examining the Opportunities and Challenges of Land Consolidation in Indian Country', 118th Congress (2023–2024). Published on *Congress.gov* website:

https://www.congress.gov/event/118th-congress/house-event/LC72726/text.

Chapter 4

1. This does not mean that all cases of outlandish or unlikely belief have this function. Many breakthroughs in scientific knowledge begin with a statement that people find hard to believe. Think of Galileo's findings about the movements of planets, moons and stars relative to the earth. The difference is that Galileo's findings were ultimately accepted because the evidence established that the claims were not outlandish after all. Indeed, it became clearly outlandish *not* to believe.
2. Jacques Jouanna, *Hippocrates* (Johns Hopkins University Press, 2001).
3. All newborns have this hole, which functions in utero to prevent blood going to the lungs. Normally, the hole closes after birth.
4. Hippocrates was preceded by pioneering developments in scientific thought by Ionian philosophers, beginning with Thales and Anaximander in the 6th century BC, in and around the Ancient Greek city-state of Miletus. See Daniel W. Graham, *Explaining the Cosmos: The Ionian Tradition of Scientific Philosophy* (Princeton University Press, 2006).
5. Source for discussion on Followers of Christ is Jason Wilson, 'Letting Them Die: Parents Refuse Medical Help for Children in the Name of Christ', *Guardian*, 14 April 2016, https://www.theguardian.com/us-news/2016/apr/13/followers-of-christ-idaho-religious-sect-child-mortality-refusing-medical-help.
6. Wilson, 'Letting Them Die'.
7. David Deutsch, *The Beginning of Infinity: Explanations That Transform the World* (Penguin, 2011), p. 212.
8. Andres E. Cruz-Inigo, Barry Ladizinski and Aisha Sethi, 'Albinism in Africa: Stigma, Slaughter and Awareness Campaigns', *Dermatologic Clinics* 29(1) (2011), pp. 79–87. Quote from p. 79. On the figure of $75,000, the authors cite International Federation of Red Cross and Red Crescent Societies, *Through Albino Eyes: The Plight of Albino People in Africa's Great Lakes Region and a Red Cross Response* (Advocacy Report, 2009).
9. Václav Havel, *The Power of the Powerless: Citizens against the State in Central-Eastern Europe* (M.E. Sharpe, 1985).
10. Harry G. Frankfurt, 'On Bullshit', *Raritan Quarterly Review* 6(2) (1986), pp. 81–100.

11 Timur Kuran, *Private Truths, Public Lies: The Social Consequences of Preference Falsification* (Harvard University Press, 1997).
12 Ian G. Baird, 'Where Do the Ravenous Spirits (*Phi Pop*) Go? Nakasang Village in Southern Laos as a Place of Cultural Healing', *Southeast Asian Studies* 13(1) (2024), pp. 109–138.
13 See Kenneth Burke, *Permanence and Change* (New Republic, 1935) and *A Grammar of Motives* (Prentice-Hall, 1945). René Girard, *The Scapegoat* (Johns Hopkins University Press, 1986).
14 Dan M. Kahan, 'Why Smart People Are Vulnerable to Putting Tribe Before Truth', *Scientific American*, 3 December 2018, https://www.scientificamerican.com/blog/observations/why-smart-people-are-vulnerable-to-putting-tribe-before-truth/.
15 Reeves Wiedeman, 'The Sandy Hook Hoax', *New York* magazine, 5 September 2016. Published on the *Intelligencer* website: http://nymag.com/daily/intelligencer/2016/09/the-sandy-hook-hoax.html. The Sandy Hook conspiracy theorists call themselves 'truthers', a word also used for those who say that the 2001 attacks on the World Trade Center were staged by the US government, or that the 1969 moon landing was broadcast from a Hollywood studio.
16 Posner set up the HONR Network to defend victims' families' right to grieve in peace and with dignity. http://www.honr.com/.
17 Wiedeman, 'The Sandy Hook Hoax'.

Chapter 5

1 Peter C. Wason, 'On the Failure to Eliminate Hypotheses in a Conceptual Task', *Quarterly Journal of Experimental Psychology* 12(3) (1960), pp. 129–140.
2 For the definitive defence of the scientific method as a process of falsification: Karl R. Popper, *The Logic of Scientific Discovery* (Hutchinson, 1959).
3 Tweet by @SenSanders, 28 January 2017: https://mobile.x.com/SenSanders/status/825004645919526912.
4 Duncan R. Lorimer, M. Bailes, M.A. McLaughlin, D.J. Narkevic, F. Crawford, 'A Bright Millisecond Radio Burst of Extragalactic Origin', *Science Magazine* 318(5851) (2007), pp. 777–780.
5 Emily Petroff, E.F. Keane, E.D. Barr, J.E. Reynolds, J. Sarkissian, … and S. Bhandari, 'Identifying the Source of Perytons at the Parkes Radio Telescope', *Monthly Notices of the Royal Astronomical Society* 451(4) (2015), pp. 3933–3940. Quote from p. 3933.
6 T.J. Hamblin, 'Fake!', *British Medical Journal* 283 (1981), pp. 1671–1674. Quote from p. 1671.

NOTES

[7] Mike Sutton, 'Spinach, Iron and Popeye: Ironic Lessons from Biochemistry and History on the Importance of Healthy Eating, Healthy Scepticism and Adequate Citation', *Internet Journal of Criminology* (2010), https://www.internetjournalofcriminology.com/_files/ugd/b93dd4_1fe4a4c3e82444d1986c4ef560a91e28.pdf.

[8] James Heathers, 'INMICE, Explained: The Serious Intent behind a Wilfully Dumb Idea', *Medium*, 16 April 2019, https://jamesheathers.medium.com/in-mice-explained-77b61b598218.

[9] Heathers, 'INMICE, Explained'.

[10] Duane Hamacher, 'The Moon Plays an Important Role in Indigenous Culture and Helped Win a Battle over Sea Rights', *The Conversation*, 12 February 2021, https://theconversation.com/the-moon-plays-an-important-role-in-indigenous-culture-and-helped-win-a-battle-over-sea-rights-119081.

[11] Hamacher, 'The Moon Plays an Important Role in Indigenous Culture'.

[12] Michael J. Balick and Gregory M. Plunkett, 'Using Plants as Calendars', *New York Botanical Garden*, 25 October 2023, https://www.nybg.org/planttalk/using-plants-as-calendars/. Many other examples show this even more vividly, such as the jacaranda trees on the University of Sydney campus. When the trees flower, students know that they should already be studying for their exams. Of course there is no causal link.

[13] Isaac Newton, *Principia Mathematica* (first published 1687) Book III, Proposition XXIV, Theorem XIX, pp. 435ff.

[14] National Ocean Service (National Oceanic and Atmospheric Administration), 'What is a King Tide?', 16 June 2024, https://oceanservice.noaa.gov/facts/kingtide.html.

[15] Newton, *Principia Mathematica*, pp. 438–439.

[16] Newton, *Principia Mathematica*, p. 436.

[17] Tony Barrass, 'Everything is Written Twice – in the Sky and on the Ground (Part Two)', *National Indigenous Times*, 6 May 2016, https://nit.com.au/06-05-2016/5/everything-written-twice-sky-ground-part-two.

[18] Ray Norris, 'Australia's First Astronomers', *BBC Earth*, no date, https://www.bbcearth.com/news/australias-first-astronomers.

[19] Hamacher, 'The Moon Plays an Important Role in Indigenous Culture'.

[20] J.D. Hays, John Imbrie and N.J. Shackleton, 'Variations in the Earth's Orbit: Pacemaker of the Ice Ages', *Science* 194(4270) (1976), pp. 1121–1132.

21 Dennis V. Kent, Paul E. Olson, Cornelia Rasmussen, Christopher Lepre, Roland Mundil, ... and William G. Parker, 'Empirical Evidence for Stability of the 405-kiloyear Jupiter–Venus Eccentricity Cycle Over Hundreds of Millions of Years', *Proceedings of the National Academy of Sciences of the United States of America* 115(4) (2018), pp. 6153–6158. See also Jonathan Horner, Pam Vervoort, Stephen R. Kane, Alma Y. Ceja, David Waltham, ... and Sandra Kirtland Turner, 'Quantifying the Influence of Jupiter on the Earth's Orbital Cycles', *The Astronomical Journal* 159(10) (2020), pp. 1–16.

22 Indeed, Newton has already been superseded – in theory – by Einstein. A key factor in that advance was the puzzling orbit of the planet Mercury, which deviates from the pattern predicted by Newton's theory. Einstein's theory of general relativity was able to explain the facts of Mercury's orbit, a demonstration that helped convince the scientific community that Einstein's theory was correct. See Richard Baum and William Sheehan, *In Search of Planet Vulcan: The Ghost in Newton's Clockwork Universe* (Springer, 1997) and G. M. Clemence, 'The Relativity Effect in Planetary Motions', *Reviews of Modern Physics* 19(4) (1947), pp. 361–364.

Chapter 6

1 William K. Clifford, 'The Ethics of Belief', *Contemporary Review* 29 (January 1877), pp. 289–309.

2 *United States v. Jewell*, 532 F.2d 697 (9th Cir. 1976). This case is described in John Kaplan, Robert Weisberg and Guyora Binder, *Criminal Law: Cases and Materials*, 7th edition (Wolters Kluwer Law & Business, 2012), p. 225.

3 *US v. Jewell* at 700–701 and nn. 4–9. See Kaplan et al, *Criminal Law*, p. 226. See also Linsey McGoey, *The Unknowers: How Strategic Ignorance Rules the World* (Bloomsbury, 2019), Chapter 9.

4 *United States v. Bronston*, 453 F.2d 555, 556 (2d. Cir. 1971), rev'd, 409 U.S. 352 (1973). This case is described on pp. 274ff of Ira P. Robbins, 'Perjury by Omission', *Washington University Law Review* 97 (2019), pp. 267–296.

5 Robbins, 'Perjury by Omission', p. 275.

6 Robbins, 'Perjury by Omission', p. 276.

7 Robbins, 'Perjury by Omission', p. 267.

8 McGoey, *The Unknowers*.

NOTES

[9] https://musiciansunion.org.uk/working-performing/orchestral-work/orchestral-auditions/screened-auditions.

[10] Office of Public Affairs, US Department of Justice, 'GlaxoSmithKline to Plead Guilty and Pay $3 Billion to Resolve Fraud Allegations and Failure to Report Safety Data', *Press Release*, 2 July 2012, https://www.justice.gov/opa/pr/glaxosmithkline-plead-guilty-and-pay-3-billion-resolve-fraud-allegations-and-failure-report.

[11] Sophie Reilly, *Animal Law Case Book* (2017), Chapter 5, Section 5.1, https://austlii.community/foswiki/Books/AnimalLawCaseBook/WebHome.

[12] Sophie Reilly, *Animal Law Case Book*.

[13] Kaplan et al, *Criminal Law*, p. 762; see also pp. 225–227.

[14] Submissions to Parliament of New South Wales Select Committee on Landowner Protection from Unauthorised Filming or Surveillance (established 17 May 2018), https://www.parliament.nsw.gov.au/committees/listofcommittees/Pages/committee-details.aspx?pk=257#tab-submissions.

[15] John Stuart Mill, *On Liberty* (Longman, Roberts, & Green Company, 1859).

[16] Hugo Mercier, *Not Born Yesterday: The Science of Who We Trust and What We Believe* (Princeton University Press, 2020), p. 206.

[17] Stephen Bayley, '20 Designs that Defined the Modern World: Number 6, London Tube Map' (no date), https://edition.cnn.com/interactive/style/20-designs-that-defined-the-modern-world/#london_tube_map. Darien Graham-Smith, 'The History of the Tube Map', *Londonist*, 6 April 2018, https://londonist.com/2016/05/the-history-of-the-tube-map.

[18] This quote is often attributed to author Stewart Brand, https://en.wikipedia.org/wiki/Information_wants_to_be_free.

[19] This is often attributed to political activist Ralph Nader, and sometimes to Thomas Jefferson. See 'Information is the Currency of Democracy (Spurious Quotation)', *Monticello*, https://www.monticello.org/research-education/thomas-jefferson-encyclopedia/information-currency-democracy-spurious-quotation/#fn-src-3.

[20] For Assange's comment that 'true information does good', see his response to an interviewer's question 'Is there anything you wouldn't leak?' starting at 00:05:42, in https://www.youtube.com/watch?v=W1IXYzJirto&t=342s

[21] Michael Schudson, 'The Right to Know vs the Need for Secrecy: The US Experience', *The Conversation*, 4 May 2015,

https://theconversation.com/the-right-to-know-vs-the-need-for-secrecy-the-us-experience-40948.

[22] Glenn Greenwald, 'Why Privacy Matters', TEDGlobal talk, October 2014, https://www.ted.com/talks/glenn_greenwald_why_privacy_matters/transcript?subtitle=en.

Chapter 7

[1] Karl Popper, *The Open Society and its Enemies* (Princeton University Press, 1945), Chapter 24. This idea was unpacked in Popper's 1987 essay, 'The Myth of the Framework': Karl Popper, 'The Myth of the Framework', in Joseph C. Pitt and Marcello Pera (eds) *Boston Studies in the Philosophy of Science* (Springer, 1976), pp. 35–62.

[2] This of course is an ideal, and self-correction requires a degree of discipline that is hard to sustain. Scientific breakthroughs typically involve correction and change of entrenched understandings, but these do not necessarily come about when individuals change their minds. Being human, scientists will often defend their ideas to the grave, a fact captured in the physicist Max Planck's famous remarks: 'A new scientific truth does not triumph by convincing its opponents and making them see the light, but rather because its opponents eventually die and a new generation grows up that is familiar with it.' Max K. Planck, *Scientific Autobiography and Other Papers* (Philosophical Library, 1950), p. 33. In other words: Science proceeds one funeral at a time.

[3] Jonathan Rauch, *Kindly Inquisitors: The New Attacks on Free Thought* (University of Chicago Press, 1994). Quotes in this paragraph are from pp. 48–49.

[4] It is important not to misunderstand this point. Undeniably, some people know better about certain matters than others. This is called expertise. We are better off, in principle, when we value expertise and trust experts. (See Tom Nichols, *The Death of Expertise*, 2nd edition [Cambridge University Press, 2024].) But valuing expertise is not the same as believing what an expert says *because they say so*. Experts are no less deserving of rigorous critique than anyone. A healthy community of error-correcting experts will ensure that no individual is getting away with unfounded or poorly evidenced claims.

[5] Jonathan Rauch, *The Constitution of Knowledge: A Defence of Truth* (The Brookings Institution Press, 2021), Chapter 1.

NOTES

[6] The term 'antifragile' is from Nassim Nicholas Taleb, *Antifragile: Things That Gain from Disorder* (Random House, 2012). It is similar to the biological principle of *hormesis*, in which a small dose of a toxin brings benefits.

[7] John Stuart Mill, *All Minus One: John Stuart Mill's Ideas on Free Speech Illustrated*, edited by Richard J. Reeves and Jonathan Haidt (Heterodox Academy, 2018), pp. 20–22.

[8] 'Noise' here does not mean unpleasant sound, but rather it refers in the more technical sense to random variation in a system.

[9] Stuart Russell and Peter Norvig, *Artificial Intelligence: A Modern Approach*, 4th edition (Pearson, 2021).

[10] Eitan Wilf, 'Contingency and the Semiotic Mediation of Distributed Agency', in N.J. Enfield and Paul Kockelman (eds) *Distributed Agency* (Oxford University Press, 2017), pp. 199–209. Quote is from p. 199.

[11] Wilf, 'Contingency', p. 202.

[12] Susan Rako, 'The "I Ching" as Facilitator in Psychotherapy', *Psychology Today*, 6 November 2016, https://www.psychologytoday.com/intl/blog/more-light/201611/the-i-ching-facilitator-in-psychotherapy.

[13] The 'culture clash' phrasing is used repeatedly by Popper in 'The Myth of the Framework'.

[14] This is one reason why innovators are often so young. Newton, Einstein and Turing were all in their twenties when they made their revolutionary breakthroughs. As Max Planck wrote, 'the future lies with the youth' (Planck, *Scientific Autobiography*, p. 97).

[15] Benjamin Lee Whorf, *Language, Thought, and Reality* (MIT Press, 2012), p. 209.

[16] Neuroscientist Erik Hoel has used the argument from overfitting to motivate a theory of why we dream. He proposes that dreams inject valuable noise into our usually dreary daily sample of information, thus counteracting cognitive overfitting. Erik Hoel, 'The Overfitted Brain: Dreams Evolved to Assist Generalization', *Patterns* 2(5) (2021), Article 100244.

[17] Teresa M. Bejan, 'A People's History of Free Speech', *Persuasion*, 10 October 2024, https://www.persuasion.community/p/a-peoples-history-of-free-speech.

[18] Teresa M. Bejan, 'The Two Clashing Meanings of "Free Speech"', *The Atlantic*, 2 December 2017, https://www.theatlantic.com/politics/archive/2017/12/two-concepts-of-freedom-of-speech/546791/.

19. William Chopik, Kim Götschi, Alejandro Carrillo, Rebekka Weidmann and Jeff Potter, 'Changes in Need for Uniqueness From 2000 Until 2020', *Collabra: Psychology* 10(1) (2024), pp. 1–10. Dennis Chong, Jack Citrin and Morris Levy, 'The Realignment of Political Tolerance in the United States', *Perspectives on Politics* 22(1) (2024), pp. 131–152.
20. Bejan, 'A People's History of Free Speech'.
21. The note called for 'a holy war against all unbelievers'. Timothy Garton Ash, *Facts are Subversive: Political Writing from a Decade Without a Name* (Atlantic Books, 2010), p. 175. See Ian Buruma, *Murder in Amsterdam: The Death of Theo van Gogh and the Limits of Tolerance* (Penguin, 2006).
22. See N.J. Enfield, *Language vs. Reality: Why Language Is Good for Lawyers and Bad for Scientists* (MIT Press, 2022), pp. 143–147, for a discussion of changes in the word 'violence' beginning in academia and spreading to public discourse.
23. Joseph Heath, 'Illiberal Liberalism', *Persuasion*, 31 July 2024, https://www.persuasion.community/p/illiberal-liberalism. See also Nick Haslam, 'Concept Creep: Psychology's Expanding Concepts of Harm and Pathology', *Psychological Inquiry* 27(1) (2016), pp. 1–17. Haslam describes the steady broadening of scope of the words listed in successive editions of the authoritative Diagnostic and Statistical Manual of Mental Disorders (DSM), such that, for example, 'trauma' once referred to direct and often catastrophic physical harm but in recent years its threshold for objective severity is lowered substantially.
24. Popper, 'Myth of the Framework', p. 37.
25. Bejan, 'A People's History of Free Speech'.
26. Bejan, 'A People's History of Free Speech'.
27. Salman Rushdie, 'Democracy is No Polite Tea Party', *Los Angeles Times*, 7 February 2005.

FURTHER READING

Julian Baggini, *A Short History of Truth* (Quercus, 2017).
David Deutsch, *The Beginning of Infinity: Explanations That Transform the World* (Penguin, 2011).
Julia Galef, *The Scout Mindset: Why Some People See Things Clearly and Others Don't* (Portfolio, 2021).
Jennifer Kavanagh and Michael D. Rich, *Truth Decay: An Initial Exploration of the Diminishing Role of Facts and Analysis in American Public Life* (RAND, 2018).
John Stuart Mill, *All Minus One: John Stuart Mill's Ideas on Free Speech Illustrated*. Edited by Richard V. Reeves and Jonathan Haidt (Heterodox Academy, 2018).
Karl R. Popper, *The Myth of the Framework: In Defence of Science and Rationality*. Edited by M.A. Notturno (Routledge, 1994).
Jonathan Rauch, *Kindly Inquisitors: The New Attacks on Free Thought* (University of Chicago Press, 1994).

INDEX

References to figures are in *italics* and references to endnotes show both the page number and the note number (110n5).

A

Achi language 21–22
actionable beliefs 36, 46–47, 48, 51
action-relevant information 92–93
Ahoe people, Laos 39–41
albinism 53–55, *54*
alignment problem xxi–xxii
ambiguous language 4–7
Animal Farm (Orwell) 35
Animal Liberation Limited 87, 90
articles of faith 30, *30*, 32–34
artificial intelligence 101–102
Assange, Julian 94
Australian Broadcasting Commission (ABC) 87, 89
Australian Pork Limited 90–91
authorities *see* cultural authorities

B

Bechet, Sidney *103*
Beck, Harry 92–93
Becket, Thomas 4, *5*, 6
Bejan, Teresa M. 108
bias-reduction measures 86
Black Hawk shootdown incident 3–4
Boghossian, Paul 23

bolas spiders 19–20
Bouyeri, Mohammed 106
Bronston, Samuel 84–85
brute (physical) reality 1–2, 27–32

C

calendar plants 72–73
Chacha, Bianca *54*
Cheyenne River Sioux 23–24, 37–38, 59
claims to knowledge 25, 36–37
  see also expertise
Clifford, William K. 21, 82–83
collateral damage 36, 43–44, 51–52
collective deception 32
colour spectrum 9–10
confidentiality 94–95
confirmation bias 17, 61–63, 83, 91
conspiracy theories 58–60
Copernicus, Nicolaus 73
court cases 7–8, 78, 83–85, 87–89
Craig, Larry 6–7
creativity 48
credulity 21
criticism 48

INDEX

cultural authorities 14, 21–25, 36–37, 39–41, 57–58

D

deniability 4–8, 86
Deutsch, David xxii–xxiii, 37
dialects, languages and 113n10
diverse information ecology 100–108
Dorze people, Ethiopia 33
Durkheim, Émile 13

E

Einstein, Albert 118n22, 121n14
Électricité de France 40
empirical rule 99
enemies of truth 97–98
England, Nora 21, 22
Enlightenment xxiii, 36–37, 106
Enlightenment thinking 98–99
equal validity doctrine 36, 37
Eucharist 30, *30*
Evans-Pritchard, E.E. 30
evidence 21, 22–23, 25, 37
expertise 37, 69–70, 120n4

F

faith healing 49–53
false beliefs 16–21, 32
falsification 61–63
Fast Radio Bursts (FRBs) 63–64, 65
Followers of Christ 49–53, *52*
Foot, Philippa 112n1
Frankfurt, Harry G. 56
free speech 105–108
freedom of information 94–95

G

Galef, Julia 17
Galileo 73, 115n1
GlaxoSmithKline 86–87
Godwin, William xxii, 80

gossip 20
government inquiries 90–91
gravity, Newton's theory of 74–76, *75*, *76*, 77–78, 79, 80
Greenwald, Glenn 95

H

half-truths 84–85
Hamblin, T.J. 66
Haslam, Nick 122n23
Havel, Václav 55–56
Heathers, James 68–69
Heider, Lee 50–51
Henry II, King of England 4, 6
hidden-camera activism 87–89, 90–91
Hippocrates 47
Hoel, Erik 121n16
Holy Communion 30, *30*
Horace xxiii
Hoyt, Brian 50

I

I Ching 103
identity signalling 32–34, 36, 43–47, 51–52, 55–57, 58–59, 108
Indigenous beliefs 12–13, 23, 30, 32–33, 37–41, 76–78
Indigenous knowledge of natural world 70–73, 76–80
intellectual humility 97–100
interview bias 86
isegoria 105

J

jazz musicians 102, *103*
Jesus Christ 44–45
Jewell, Charles 83

K

Kahan, Dan M. 58
Kant, Immanuel xxiii, 106

Kelly, John 87–89
Khamsone, Mrs 39–41, *39*
K'ichee' language 21–22
Kinyanjui, Gabriel *54*
Knight, Chris 32
Kri people, Laos 32–33
Kuran, Timur 57

L

land-rights claims 23–24, 37–41
language, ambiguities in 4–7
language, bluntness of 9–10, 13–14
language, central role of 1–2, 8–9
language, triangulation through 10–11, 27–28
language, word meanings 2–4
language games 35
language learning 104–105
languages, dialects and 113n10
Laos xxi–xxii, 10, 13–14, 16–17, 32–34, 35–36, 39–41
LeBeau, Ryman 37–38, *38*
LeBeau, Sebastian 23
legal cases 7–8, 78, 83–85, 87–89
Lenah Game Meats 87–89
Lévi-Strauss, Claude 114n7
liberal science 98–99
literal truth defence 85
London tube map 92–93, *93*
Lorimer, Duncan R. 64
Louis XIV, King of France xx

M

machine-learning algorithms 101–102
McGinn, Colin 110n5
meat industry 87–89, 90–91, 94
medical science 47–53
Mill, John Stuart 91, 100, 106
mindful optimism 97–109
mistaken beliefs 16–21, 32
Moon Dance 78

moon landings 43–44
moon phases 70–72, 73–80, *75*, *76*
moths, mating pheromones 19–20
Mwaura, Isaac *54*
mysterianism xxiii

N

Nam Theun 2 hydroelectricity project 39–41
Narkevic, David J. 64
nature, forces of xx–xxi, xxii–xxiv, 42
neap tides 71, 76
New South Wales Government Select Committee on Landowner Protection from Unauthorised Filming or Surveillance 90–91
Newton, Isaac 74–76, *75*, *76*, 77–78, 79, 80, 121n14
Norris, Ray 77–78
Nuer people, Sudan 30

O

optimistic reasoning xxii–xxiii
see also mindful optimism
orchestra auditions 86, 94
Orwell, George 35
Ostrich Instruction 83–84, 89
overfitting 101–105

P

Parkes Observatory 64, 65–66
parrhesia 105
peer review 86
perpetual improvement doctrine xxii, 80–81
perytons 65–66
Petroff, Emily 65
physical (brute) reality 1–2, 27–29, 31–32

INDEX

Planck, Max K. 120n2, 121n14
Popeye 66, 67, 67
Popper, Karl P. 98–99, 100, 107
possum slaughtering 87–89
Pozner, Len 60
Pozner, Noah 58–59, 60
preference falsification 57
privacy 94–95

Q

questioning in court 7–8, 83–85
Quod gratis asseritur, gratis negatur 37

R

Rako, Susan 103
rationalism 98–108
rationality 98–99
Rauch, Jonathan 98–99
reasons for action 16–20, 84, 95–96
relativity, Einstein's theory of 118n22
religious beliefs 30, 30, 32, 33–34, 43–47, 49–53
Rule Discovery Test 61–62
Rushdie, Salman 108

S

Sanders, Bernie 63
Sandy Hook Elementary School shooting 58–60
Sapere aude xxiii
sceptical rule 99
Schudson, Michael 94
science, trust in 69–70
science reporting 68–69
scientific errors 64–68
scientific explanation 72–80
scientific method 61–64
scientific mindset xxiii, 36–37, 47–49, 53, 81
  see also mindful optimism

scout analogy 17
sea rights claims 78
Searle, John R. 1, 29
secrecy, need for 94–95
selective knowledge 82–84, 86–89, 91–95
Shahadah 32
signalling beliefs 32–34, 36, 43–47, 51–52, 55–57, 58–59, 108
Signorini, Chiara 24, 37, 57
Sis Iboy, Nikte' 21–23
Snook, Scott A. 111n4
social bonding 43–46
social motivations 20
  see also identity signalling
social reality 28–32, 41–42
social symbolism 33–34
soldier mindset 17, 25–26
Somin, Ilya 21
Sperber, Dan 33
spinach-iron story 64–65, 66–68
spring tides 71, 75
status function declarations 29–30
strategic unknowing 82–84, 85
supernatural beliefs 13–14, 23, 24–25, 32–33, 37–41, 43–47, 49–50, 53–55, 76–78, 114n7
Sutton, Mike 66–67, 68

T

Tanna island, Vanuatu 72–73
Tarski, Alfred 2
tide cycles 70–72, 73–80, 75, 76
Torres Strait Islanders 70–72, 78, 80
totem identity 12–14
toxic plants xxi–xxii
triangulation 10–11, 27–28
tribe before truth 58, 109
truth conditions 2

U

Ultima ratio naturae xx–xxi, 42
Ultima ratio regum xx–xxi, 42
uncomfortable truths 91–92
US military 3–4

V

van Gogh, Theo 106–107
Vanuatu 72–73
Vietnam War 92

W

Walton, Mariah 49–50
Wason, Peter 61–62
Weber, Max 31
Whorf, Benjamin Lee 104–105
Wilf, Eitan 102
wilful blindness 82–84, 89
witchcraft accusations 24–25, 25, 37, 57–58
withholding information 84–89
Wittgenstein, Ludwig 35
Wolf, Emil von 65, 66–68
Wolf of Wall Street (film) 5–6
World Bank 40

Y

Yolngu people, Arnhem Land, Australia 76–78

www.ingramcontent.com/pod-product-compliance
Lightning Source LLC
Jackson TN
JSHW021800080925
90677JS00005B/29